MW00928061

Advancing in
Yoga

The path of Kundalini, the chakras and the Siddhas

Nacho Albalat, Nityananda

Copyright © 2020 Nacho Albalat, Nityananda
email: info@kriyayogadebabaji.net

ISBN: 9798641620374
Imprint: Independently published

All rights reserved. No part of this book may be reproduced
or utilized in any form or by any means, electronic or
mechanical, including photocopying, recording, or by any
information storage and retrieval system, without permission
in writing from the publisher..

Contents

Advancing in
Yoga

The path of Kundalini, the chakras and
the Siddhas

Introduction

"Yoga" is union, union with the Self. This union is impossible without going through a process of transformation. In the Yoga of the Siddhas this transformation process includes the physical, vital, mental, intellectual and spiritual dimensions. It also requires guidance. Guidance includes clearly describing the stages in the process and how success in realizing goals can be evaluated. While this book was originally aimed at advanced students of Babaji's Kriya Yoga, any Yoga student engaged in his transformation process can also benefit from reading it. To provide such guidance is the purpose of this book. It is based upon my personal experience in practicing Babaji's Kriya Yoga for the past 25 years.

Before writing this book I had a dream: *I was facing the closed doors of an exhibition hall about immortal yogis. The enclosure doors were closed. Inside, a guide guided the visitors and explained the meaning and history of the different objects displayed there. Then the doors opened and we were able to enter the exhibition and contemplate all the objects. But now there was no guide. But the same objects were there, within reach of whoever wanted to see them. But there was no explanation about them.*

My interest, as a yogi and as a former journalist now focused on spreading yogic knowledge, is to help practitioners of this path by providing clarity about the goals, and also the challenges, of an advanced practice of Yoga. The kriyas or techniques of the Siddhas are represented by the objects of the exposition of my dream. What is required is some written guidance on their context, their meaning and their purpose. The purpose of this book is to offer that guide, as far as possible.

This book talks about how to approach the process of personal transformation that is activated and accelerated by yogic kriyas and the intense practice. A process that, I believe, every student committed to Yoga and spirituality must experience, sooner or later.

For those who do not follow the path of Babaji's Kriya Yoga, I have included various yogic techniques that can help you on the path that you are already following. You can do any of these practices, the ones that resonate with you, in the order and at the time you want. Discover the results and benefits that they produce in you. They are simple but can generate powerful results, and become part of your daily yogic practice if you wish. You can write to me if you have any questions.

I hope that with these texts, people committed to a growth process through Yoga can advance more and better on the path.

Jai Guru.

Nacho Albalat, Nityananda

info@ kriyayogadebabaji.net
www.kriyayogadebabaji.net

Sadhana: Creating the inner space of Self

The purpose of *sadhana* or spiritual practice is to create an internal space of consciousness and bliss that does not depend on external circumstances. To create that space, you need to do an internal cleansing. This internal cleansing occurs through the practice of yogic kriyas.

Life is in perpetual change. You cannot control the external reality; you can do the best you can, but you do not control the results of your actions. You can, however, always take care of the contents of your inner space.

Sadhana is a process of purification and cleansing of the mind, the contents of inner space. First you get emptied of all the limiting and unnecessary contents. Then that space is filled with the Self. The Self is pure and blissful consciousness. Babaji is the incarnation of the grace of the Self, guiding and inspiring individuals towards Himself. "The jiva becomes Shiva" is one of the great sayings of the Siddhas: the individual becomes the Divine. Yoga is what makes possible this process of transformation.

The sadhana of the Siddhas

Let's imagine that our inner space is like a house, metaphorically. In the house which is inhabited by someone practicing classical Yoga, the yogi often climbs upwards to the spiritual dimension, represented in this metaphor as the roof, on a ladder consisting of the eight steps of yoga until finally departing into the sky. The classical yogi seeks the Divine beyond this world with its endless cycles of reincarnation born of desire.

In the Kriya Yoga of the Siddhas we are not going anywhere. We are dedicated to cleansing and emptying the rooms of our house, so that little by little there is more light and more space in them. From time to time we are ecstatic to see an empty room, clean and full of light. And then we discover how much more we have to clean, and then we proceed to resume the cleaning work. With time and practice, our house is becoming a place of space and light, and in that light - which has always been there, but we never saw it because the house was so full and dirty - we discover the Divine there, which becomes the inhabitant of our home.

Siddhas perceive the Siva-loka here;
They experience within nada[1] and Nadanta.[2]
They are eternal, pure and blemishless;
Liberated are they, from the tattvas thirty-six[3].

- Tirumandiram, verse 125[4]

In our spiritual practice we have not gone anywhere; we have cleansed the personal space where we are, daring to clean our entire house, including its darkest corners, letting go of its contents.

The Siddhas speak of "vettaveli," the vast, luminous space of liberation.

In Yoga it is considered that the human being has five sheaths or koshas, each of them more subtle than the previous one: physical, emotional or vital, mental, intellectual and causal bodies. **The path of the Siddhas is that of the transmutation of these five sheaths, from abodes of karma to temples where the Divine resides and manifests**. The five sheaths are transformed into recipients capable of housing the Divine. The path of the Siddhas is not a way of transcendence of this world, but a way of self-transformation, even physical transformation:

Recipients are they, in this world, of the great way;
Recipients are they, in this world, of the reward of

birthlessness;
Recipients are they of the boon of eternal closeness;
Recipients are they of the power of silence in the world.

- Tirumandiram, verse 132

Presence and Love: the beginning and the end of the spiritual path

The beginning of the yogic process, its course and its end is the same: **you are present, blissful and loving consciousness**, independent of all the phenomena and events that come and go. The yogic realization is to establish oneself permanently in this experience.

We experience thoughts, feelings and perceptions - but we are nothing of the sort. We are aware of them and we experience them as changing phenomena, knowing that they are not our real nature, as changing clouds cannot affect the nature of the sun that illuminates them.

To the realized yogi, every phenomenon experienced is like Kali dancing above Shiva. The realized yogi, now identified with universal consciousness, Shiva, observes the dance of "Mother Nature" without being touched nor affected by it even in the slightest manner.

To perceive this is the beginning of the spiritual path, and to realize it continuously is its end. This is the center of our yogic aspiration and our understanding of the Essential Reality.

And whenever you are disturbed by transient phenomena remember what your essential nature is: blissful consciousness.

● Practice: Contemplation on Presence and Love ●

After sitting comfortably, be relaxed present, focus on the moment. Consider that your real nature is this presence that you are. Thoughts, perceptions, feelings that come and go are manifested on it. But consider and realize that you are not these phenomena, but the presence that observes them.

Take your time. Notice how joy appears when you are present, an unconditional joy that does not depend on anything external. Notice how it arises from your plexus. Let it expand through your being.

Consider how joy appears from pure presence. And watch how, united with joy, unconditional love arises, love without effort.

Consider what it would be like to live forever in this state.

This is your real nature according to Yoga.

1- *Nada*: the divine sound, Om.
2- *Nadanta*: that which is beyond the divine sound.
3- *Tattvas*: the elements that configure Nature.
4- Tirumular Siddhar. (2010). *The Tirumandiram*. St. Etienne de Bolton, Québec. Babaji´s Kriya Yoga and Publications.

The Witness and attunement with the Satguru: two basic practices for the yogi

Yoga can be defined as the scientific art of perfect God Truth union. It includes identifying with what I truly am, and ceasing to identify with what I am not. Thus, in Babaji's Kriya Yoga removing the ego's misidentification applies two practices, which eventually become constant:

- The practice of constant awareness or the Heart Witness.

- The attunement with the Satguru - Babaji.

Cultivating both aspects is necessary to grow in the realization of Self, as we will see below.

The practice of awareness

The practice of continuous awareness, also called *Nityananda Kriya*, involves constantly anchoring ourselves in the consciousness of the Heart Witness, who unconditionally observes everything that happens, inside and outside. This means not identifying with what one is not: thoughts, feelings, perceptions, experiences. All these come and go, as impermanent phenomena appearing and disappearing according to the laws of Nature. By adopting this new perspective the yogi transcends the spectacle of life, with its dualities of suffering and pleasure.

As we abandon our identification with the impermanent dualities, we identify more and more with the Self, with the absolute reality, that never changes, that is timeless. The egoistic perspective is like entering a room while walking backwards, looking at what you leave behind, instead of looking where you are going. But as one ceases to dwell on the past we enter the room of the Self in the present moment. Then there is unconditional joy, joy without object, not related to any experience, as rays of the sun that break on through the clouds of our ordinary reality. This joy is the joy of Self, and it is a blissful place to live in.

When we are not there, we are usually identifying ourselves with the experiences of the vital or emotional body, the mental or the physical bodies.

The emotional or vital body is like a horse whose owner must try to control it with sticks and carrots. This body constantly pursues emotional compensations in food, relationships, entertainments that we like... or tries to avoid what it dislikes or fears. Liking and disliking is the disease of the mind, born in memories, expressed as impulses through the vital body and into the physical body.

In Yoga we change the point of view and settle ourselves in the witness, the Seer according to the words of Siddha Patanjali. The pursuit of the pleasure of the senses ceases to be our vital motivation, but, in return, we are discovering the joy of now, the unconditional joy of Self. This process of transition from our identification with the emotional body to our identification with the Witness is gradual, and it may not be an easy process. Sometimes the vital rebels; being the one who provides us with energy, it can sometimes say, "If you don't do what I like and desire, I won't give you energy." The vital interprets as a loss the abandonment of the activities in which until now we put all our energy. But then it gets used to the change. It is necessary then to have patience, and to continue advancing little by little in the yogic practice.

Attunement with the Satguru

Through the practice of awareness we stop identifying with what we are not, the passing spectacle of life. This liberation produces joy. And from there, what? Becoming a joyful witness to everything that happens is not all there is. As Krishna points out in the Bhagavad Gita, in our life we cannot stop acting. We all have a dharma, a task or a purpose to perform in our incarnation. We need to tune into the higher Being, the Divinity, to receive inspiration to understand and perform it, and to guide our actions.

In the meditations taught in the first initiation of Kriya Yoga we learn to receive inspiration to improve our life, which culminates in the seventh meditation, in which we receive the guidance of Kriya Babaji, the Satguru and source of Kriya Yoga. "God, the guru and the Self itself are the same" say the Siddhas. It means that there is only One. Being, Consciousness and Bliss is the essence of all three. From these meditation kriyas we can learn to develop attunement with the Higher Consciousness, personified by Babaji, so that more and more grace can be obtained in our lives. Babaji is the accessible form of the Absolute – as all the satgurus are. A true satguru are thresholds, doors through which Grace manifests. There is no more valuable treasure that they on earth.

The satguru does not need the worship of anyone. What is required by the student is "attunement." This constant attunement or connection is what allows the disciple to receive the inspiration, grace and energy of the Satguru, and that allows them to act in one's life. Here the difference is established between an ordinary life and a life full of "grace", which manifests itself in small things and, sometimes, also in extraordinary things, all in due course.

The Yoga of the Siddhas, in its most advanced stages, points to a transformation even in a physical level. This final transformation is not possible only with personal effort, it requires the grace and intervention of a higher and dynamic Divine aspect. Referring to this aspect, Sri Aurobindo spoke of the Divine Mother; Ramalinga Swami spoke of the "divine light of grace", Tirumular spoke of the descent of the grace of Shiva. Yogi Ramaiah spoke of the grace of Babaji, as the result of our previous surrender to Him. Even in these last realizations, total attunement is the basis for the action of this transforming Grace.

A personal and collective transformation

The joy of the Heart Witness is an impersonal joy, the joy of Self. The attunement with the Satguru, Babaji in Kriya Yoga, is a personal vibration that implies a shakti (energy) of renewing Grace.

Both practices are necessary. If we keep ourselves in the Heart Witness we won't be dragged by the dualities of life. If, besides that, we also tune in with the Satguru, we will also feel fulfilled. Simple attunement with the Satguru without the witness consciousness prevents the student from confronting the ego and its obstacles, which will be experienced as threats to that attunement, but will not be faced or managed.

We have seen that with the constant practice of the witness we avoid identification with what we are not, and with the practice of attunement, we identify with the Satguru, our Higher Self - our real being. These are the two wings of Kriya Yoga. With them, with their constant observance, our daily life becomes our Yoga, our process of growth in the Self.

All of us are currently facing tremendous social and ecological challenges. But we cannot face them effectively without changing the state of consciousness that generates them. Through these two yogic practices we can become instruments through which a Higher Consciousness can act in our world, for the benefit of all beings.

Presence and Love: developing the Heart Witness

Behind your thoughts, feelings and perceptions there is a joyful presence - an unconditional witness who is always in joy, 24 hours a day.

You are the blissful presence, the joy of Self. To find it, you must look for it among your experience.

The Heart Witness

You focus on the witness from the heart. From there you can observe and confront feelings and thoughts of your inner space, while also experiencing the unconditional bliss that appears.

From the Heart Witness you observe what happens in the physical, emotional and vital bodies, as if they were not yours and if they had "things" in them, things that you look at with curiosity and without judging. And it really is like that; they appear, but not your real Self.

Cultivate the presence and love and confront everything from the Witness. Bring the Heart Presence to all the contents you experience. Become aware of the emotional nucleus that generate mental images and emotional states - none of them should escape from your consciousness, to the last corner of your inner space. The Heart Presence can dissolve them. Never let the mind be carried away when you experience intense emotions. Breathe, take a step back and look at it. Cultivate mental silence and presence over the emotions; let the energy of the plexus rise by unconditional observation, without categorizing it, until it is integrated. Never let that energy get entangled with mental images.

The mind uses time to perpetuate itself. It likes to dwell in the past or in the future. Being present in the now quiets the mind.

Emotions, on the other hand, intensify in the present moment. They lose their force however, when they simply become the object of our awareness. The more we are present the more both mind and emotions diminish, and unconditional joy arises.

Bring everything into the light of awareness as an offering to the Self. The Heart Presence can transmute everything, based on consciousness and love. Invoke the Satguru, Babaji, because his consciousness and love are unlimited.

By cultivating presence and love everything is confronted with the witness, and things pass through one's experience. Transcend mind and emotions by being totally present is a path of liberation.

Every moment you have is an opportunity to anchor yourself in the Heart Witness and in its joy, the joy of being, transcending mind and emotions (and transforming them when performing this practice). If you are in the Self, you are where you should be. The Heart Witness at a given moment can expand towards omnipresence; at another moment the joy of the Being can arise within.

The witness is presence and love. Babaji is presence and love. "Seek Babaji to become Babaji" said Yogi Ramaiah. When you focus on presence and love in the heart you are in the Self, you are in Babaji.

Everything that the intense practice of Kriya Yoga brings out in the light of consciousness must be transmuted into presence and love.

"I am Presence and Love" is a good affirmation to repeat throughout the sadhana and throughout the day, so you remember your Self. Everything that is not that can be considered an addition; it is not the reality of your Self.

All the yogic kriyas we practice support this process of inner cleaning and transformation, at all our five levels of manifestation: physical, vital, mental, intellectual, causal. As sadhaks of the Yoga of the Siddhas we are in a process of inner cleansing and transformation of ourselves.

Constantly practice Presence and Love until they are definitively anchored in your nature. This amounts to the realization of Self. **This is the basis to build your sadhana of Yoga.** And from this firmly established base you can effectively develop the most advanced kriyas, which will deepen and expand this realization.

Bringing the Heart Witness to the emotional body

Classical Yoga seeks as a goal the liberation from the endless cycle of reincarnations. Kriya Yoga of the Siddhas seeks the divinization of all life.

To progress on the path of the Siddhas an intensive emotional cleansing or *tapas* is needed in the fire and light of the Heart Witness.

The sadhaka must learn to purify each emotion, not by encouraging or suppressing them but by allowing them to melt into the fire and light of Self awareness. They are transformed in the melting pot of Yoga, like base metals into gold.

Hence we see the need to constantly anchor ourselves in the consciousness of the witness. From there, and from the space of bliss created by the witness, we can confront all the different emotional strata, which must be released until we get a pure emotional body, transparent to the Self.

Abide in the Self, from there observe the not self

Sometimes, the greater the resistance to change by our lower vehicles, the physical, emotional and mental bodies, the stronger the blessing received in meditation. Kriya Yoga seeks the transformation of these bodies into vehicles of the Self. The greatest battlefield for this change is often the emotional body, whose transformation can finally manifest itself in physical transformation.

Expand the witness until there is no mental or emotional movement left in you without the Presence fully observing it. The Siddhas clear the vital body of emotional movements before bringing awareness into the cells of the physical body. The process of transformation of the the emotional and vital bodies includes pranayama to a large extent The more we remove emotional tendencies and habits from our subconscious mind, the freer we become from suffering even if we temporarily feel bad when they emerge into our consciousness.

The Heart Witness must always be there, integrating the emotional and dismantling its contents, which can be traced to habits of several lives. You should not be afraid of what memories they reveal, but observe, accept and let go of them. You have survived your past. Congratulations! Now turn the page and move forwards. The emotional and the world reflect your internal contents as immovable realities of destiny, and they are not. You are not the emotions. You are the Witness. Observe what happens as a *maya* or temporary delusion woven by one's mind, instead of believing that this is an immovable reality. The subconscious must be cleaned, that is the yogic challenge of the path of the Siddhas. **Where there is suffering there is a subconscious mind that needs cleansing**.

When negative mental images are fired, focus the Heart Witness into the internal energy that triggers those thoughts. Do not let the mind put images to that energy; feel it, witness it from the Witness, without feeding it. In doing so, after a while, you will notice a change of vibration and a release of energy in the present.

Transmuting all the contents and emotional states into a joyful presence is an achievement that is achieved with a constant and tireless practice that takes time. The result is to establish the bliss, the real nature of the Self, in our lives, perhaps almost definitively. When you develop the Witness to the end, the Witness becomes everything.

Identifying emotional hubs

We should never fear any emotion, whatever it may be. All emotions are nothing but chemical elements dancing inside us. Do not be afraid of fear, or feel sad about sadness. All emotions are objects of observation for the Heart Witness; however powerful these emotions may be, there is always a part of us, however small, that is not automatically dragged by them. This part is our Self.

Thoughts give rise to emotional reactions, and sometimes it is the other way around, emotional patterns rooted in our mind give rise to thoughts. The Heart Witness must observe both.

Sometimes there are hubs or emotional contents that generate a series of thoughts. Imagine someone who is afraid of flying in a plane, and as he does, he cannot stop imagining scenes of air accidents. Or when a person has great sexual desire and does not stop imagining erotic scenes. Sometimes we experience a barrage of thoughts on a particular subject, but behind them there is a strong emotional association. Instead of wasting time with these thoughts, it is more effective to identify and confront their emotional origin, for example, fear, dissatisfaction, and sadness.

In the subconscious we have several basic hubs that generate emotions and negative thoughts. These hubs are a source of fear, dissatisfaction, sadness ... all kinds of suffering and limitations.

Instead of constantly struggling with negative recurring thoughts that arise, it is better to become aware of the subconscious hubs that generate them. As we move forward in sadhana we can identify them, and even make a list of each of these negative hubs that affect us.

The fundamental importance of mastering detachment

First, we eliminate all the images and thoughts that create discomfort for us.

Then we focus on the emotional origin that generates them, a confusing group of feelings that seem independent of us and which are probably rooted in our subconscious. We apply Presence and Love to this origin.

It is very important to strengthen, through repeated practice, the power of the Witness, to be able to accept conflicting thoughts and feelings without being dragged by them, without yielding to their proposals. All of them are not the Self but changing phenomena of nature.

To develop this muscle of the Witness it is very important the practice and mastery of the first meditation technique, Shuddi or detachment. It is the foundation on which we build our practice. The mastery of detachment not only of thoughts, but also and especially of feelings and subliminal contents, must be achieved to advance in the path.

The mastery of detachment towards conflicting emotions is especially important, as taught in the second initiation of Kriya Yoga. The sadhaka must keep in mind that these conflicting emotions must be accepted (accepting that they are there) before practicing detachment from them. **Detachment is to recognize that you are not going to put more energy into something, neither to repress it nor to recreate it.**

Detachment, correctly done, set the sadhaka free as no other practice does; the sadhaka is set free in pure consciousness. Due to habit we think that our emotions are necessary, even the conflicting ones, but they and our thoughts are simply superfluous in the face of the pure and joyful consciousness of the Self.

When the sadhaka gets free from the identification with the moods of the emotional body, he begins to feel the joy of Self everywhere, naturally.

A long and dedicated practice of detachment or *Shuddi Dhyana* is important, in addition to releasing internal contents, to create in the sadhaka the habit and inner strength of non-identification, from his full consciousness, with mental, emotional and sensory contents.

Cultivating the right thoughts

When the sadhaka is faced with undesirable emotional patterns already settled it is good to sow their opposite patterns, repeating positive affirmations that counteract them. "*When bound by negative thoughts, their opposite ones should be cultivated*" - Yoga Sutras II.33.[1]

We can finally identify all the patterns that limit us to counteract them and disarm them. We begin thus to dismantle the framework that sustains our ego, our false self based on the limitation that usurps the blissful experience of the Self.

We must realize that if our habitual thoughts are negative and limiting, they will generate equally negative and limiting emotional responses in the vital. All our thoughts generate an effect; when they are negative, we are the first to suffer their repercussions on our emotional body, which also affect our physical body and our personal happiness. We cannot let our emotional body be at the mercy of our random thoughts, especially those negative ones that trigger emotional responses at the moment without being able to avoid it. When this happens, our emotions are in the hands of the first stupid thought that crosses our mind.

And we must also realize that if we usually cultivate this type of thoughts, our emotional body won't have many options to choose. The origin of our unhappiness is not then in our vital but in the negative thoughts we usually harbor.

So the first step to transmute the emotional body into a body of peace and joy is to become aware of the thoughts that we generate, taking care of them. You can see more about it in the chapter "Identifying useless thoughts."

With the development of the Witness, there comes a time when the sadhaka can identify and dissolve the thoughts that arise in the mind before they can involve and affect the emotional body, just as one can extinguish a small flame from a match before it can burn a forest.

Equally important is also to choose properly the emotional

food we eat through our senses: books, television, movies, and internet. We are currently bombarded with an excess of information everywhere, something that did not happen centuries ago and much less in the ancient India of the yogis. We must question how much of this information that comes to us and that we follow is really necessary and inspiring for our practice and for our life, or if it drags our emotional in opposite directions towards the progress we seek.

The practice of contentment

Contentment is a yogic virtue mentioned by Siddha Patanjali in his Yoga Sutras, whose practice can help us to pacify our emotions: *"By contentment, supreme joy is gained"* - Yoga Sutras, II.42.

Contentment means accepting personal circumstances and being happy with what one has. This yogic virtue does not abound in our current society, which constantly encourages us to endless consumerism to obtain happiness. Contentment involves the cultivation of equanimity in the face of the setbacks that existence brings us, and practicing simplicity in our way of life. The development of contentment facilitates the establishment of peace.

There is a fundamental Yoga practice that everyone can do, as you will always find time for it: try to keep calm, no matter what happens, no matter what the mind, the controller of everything, says. Try it and see. Especially in situations that ask you to be overwhelmed. Decide to be at peace, against all odds, in a situation that normally overwhelms you; challenge everything and see what happens. Perhaps then you can glimpse that there is a part of you that is not beyond, but above all that happens - something like the sun that illuminates everything but is not affected by what it illuminates. And although the clouds sometimes cover it, it is there. That is the beginning of everything. Practicing unconditional calm and perceiving that part (the Self) is a practice that can keep you entertained for the rest of your life, and you will discover that the effort done it is definitely worthwhile.

Magnify peace and joy, not disappointment

In addition to cultivating the Witness, in the purification and transformation of the emotional body we can adopt a more active role. Sri Aurobindo suggests this method to transform the emotional body:

"If you get peace, then to clean the vital becomes easy. If you simply clean and clean and do nothing else, you go very slowly – for the vital gets dirty again and has to be cleaned a hundred times. Peace is something that is clean in itself, so to get it is a positive way to securing your object. To look for dirt only and clean is the negative way."[2]

Instead of only relying on changing moods of the vital and constantly following them from the Witness, we can actively promote peace and joy, until they develop as everyday habits. We can nurture our emotional body with the peace and inner joy resulting from our yogic practices, and cultivate them consciously, instead of relying on insecure and changing external circumstances to experience that joy.

1- Govindan, M. (2010). *Kriya Yoga Sutras of Patanjali and the Siddhas: Translation, Commentary and Practice.* St. Etienne de Bolton, Quebec: Babaji's Kriya Yoga and Publications.

2- Sri Aurobindo. (2003) *The integral Yoga.* Twin Lakes, USA: Lotus Press. p. 254.

Identifying useless thoughts

In my early practice of Babaji's Kriya Yoga I was able to experience joyful and peaceful states of mental silence, but only momentarily, due to the intrusion of thoughts, and often painful thoughts. But then, that is what the mind does. The mind is a great tool for reasoning and analyzing; it helps to solve problems and create realities however it also creates problems and situations that we do not want to experience. Knowing how to concentrate the mind is important for life, but we also need to learn how to cleanse and widen it into awareness.

"*I think therefore I am,*" declared the French philosopher Descartes. In the East, the Siddha Patanjali declared "*Yoga is the cessation of the fluctuations arising within consciousness, then the Seer abides in his own true form or nature*" (Yoga Sutras I.2-3). This is a radical change of perspective, which brings unconditional joy, as one realizes how to differentiate the movements of the mind, including sensations, emotions and thoughts from consciousness. We are not the thoughts; we have thoughts that come and go. But we are not what we think. We are the consciousness, that observes thoughts, and which is always present. In fact, consciousness is the only thing that has always been present throughout all of the moments of our lives. Everything else in our life is subject to change. Absolute Being, Consciousness and Bliss, is who we truly are, according to the Yoga Siddhas.

Trying to stop the mind is like trying to hold water between our hands. "*The mind never stops, impetuous, self-determined, difficult to tame... Taking control over my mind seems as difficult as appeasing the powerful winds*" says Arjuna in the *Bhagavad Gita* (VI.34). Fighting with the mind to stop it is not an effective practice. A better strategy is to observe it as a witness, without getting involved in it. The book *The Voice of Babaji: Trilogy on Kriya* Yoga declares the following about the mind:

When we just begin to reflect to trace its source, it vanishes away. If we stoop to follow it, it tries to conquer us. It does not obey us, if we obey it. If we are the Witness, merely an onlooker, noticing its rises and its falls, it cannot but become submissive to us. We are to be unconcerned with it and work in us the attitude of an unaffected witness.[1]

Normal day-to-day thoughts can be grouped into several categories. Many are useful, but also many are useless and distressful. I found that by recognizing these different categories and how they work, I have been able to rid myself of the grip that the negative ones have had on me.

I invite you to read through the following categorization of recurring thoughts. My strategy is not to resist thoughts, but to recognize them for what they are, as soon as they appear, and to immediately let them go. I compare this process to being at a party and recognizing a person who is very tiresome, someone who always repeats the same stories. You see him, recognize him and avoid engaging with him, just that. The more you do this with habitual and useless thoughts, the quicker they will lose their power to grab you and hold onto your attention.

- *Thoughts from the past:* memories that bring up negative emotions. Thoughts that linger within, tinged with fear, anger, resentment or vengeance for things done to you or guilt, repentance, embarrassment for something you did.

The past steals the present! Looking backward, creates a very heavy load preventing you from looking forward. Attending to your past, distorts and limits your vision of the present. Don't allow the mind to define you by your past. Once your lessons are learned, you don't need to repeat them. The lessons of the past, like food that you have eaten, must be digested. Once digested, each new day can be fresh, free and full of possibility.

Digestion of the past means to realize that thoughts of the past are personal, biased interpretations about what really happened. You must observe the old thought, identify it as memory, noticing its emotional charge without letting it affect you. Then, you let it go more easily. It may take a while to let go of the emotion but continue the process. Perhaps, look on a negative memory, as if it were a hoax, a mere ghost that exists only in the mind.

- *Thoughts about the future:* there are two, especially annoying thoughts of this kind:

1) fearful anticipation: when you visualize something negative that could happen in the future, adding fear to it. You do not know what tomorrow will bring! How many times, a certain future was not as you imagined? When things ended up being much better, than anticipated? Some people use fear as a vital strategy, visualizing what can go wrong and then struggling so that it does not happen. This is an emotionally exhausting strategy that make life full of anguish! Living without fear, seems scary, because the ego thinks that you must live in survival mode in order to be able to control things in your life.

Although it is appropriate to plan well for the future, it is more important to identify and release these fearful thoughts as soon as they appear, so that they do not grip the mind and emotions. A better strategy, to avoiding what you do not want to happen, is to visualize positively what you really want to create, and put your energy there.

2) exhaustion by anticipation: this second type is when you think about what you have to do, tomorrow, this week or in the future, and allow yourself to be overwhelmed by feelings of fatigue, inadequacy, or despondency. Better to live one day at a time engaged fully and contentedly in what there is to do today. Instead of identifying with the frequency of the mind to judge every situation, identify with the presence of the witness. Anticipation takes us away from the present, the witness, the only thing that exists and the only thing we have. "Sufficient to the day is the trouble thereof" - even as every hour has its own. If you observe you will see that each day has its own opportunities for learning. The lessons and preoccupations change over time and are replaced by new ones. So as soon as

one of these thoughts appears, discard it knowing that "tomorrow will be another day". One day at a time is enough.

Remember that thoughts of the past - usually accompanied by feelings of shame, pain or remorse - and thoughts of the future - usually accompanied by fear or stress - are the mind's resource to get you out of the fullness of now. When these thoughts come, ignore them as constructs of the ego and use them as reminders to practice Witness awareness and joyful Presence.

- *Thoughts of desire or aversion:* when an image of an object of desire or enjoyment arises, along with fantasy about how happy you will be, when you are able to get it. The mind imagines that you will be happy once you attain whatever it is you desire, sex, a specific meal, an expensive purchase, whatever, it may be. The mind is disturbed by your decision that you must have this. Or, on the other hand, the opposite distraction is a reoccurring thought that involves aversion, something you do not want. Your mind, disturbed by apprehension, perhaps fear can become obsessed in avoiding whatever this is.

Desire is the base, they say in India, of Creation. But the Siddhas remind us that desire makes us forget the true unconditional bliss or ananda, the joy of the Self. All desires are poor substitutes, in comparison, with this Ananda. The mind makes us both want things and reject things, and these perpetuate themselves due to the ego. But when we experience the ananda of just being, dualities disappear. Desire and aversions dissolve. Everything becomes neutral. It is fine either way.

It is interesting to then, observe the thoughts of desire, how the objects of desire are sweetened and made attractive by your mind, and how their final satisfaction differs greatly from your original fantasy about them, or how short-lived satisfaction lasts. For the mind, if left on its own, will generate another new desire before you know it. Look deeply and discover just how often your mind deludes you with things that do not last, and how you still are dominated by it.

- *Thoughts about your own worth and acceptance/respect of others:* As children, we develop strategies to achieve the attention, recognition and affection of our authorities and others. We learn to be entertaining, witty, polite, or quiet and respectful? What is your strategy when interacting with others? Sometimes past conditioning from childhood creates monsters of mental thoughts and strategies that can sabotage our sense of self-worth and self-respect, self-confidence. We perhaps experience restlessness, jealousy, pride, defensiveness, and have a general lack of confidence. The mind plays with us but we don't know we are playing a game with it. are playing the game of the mind of the search for recognition and acceptance. Recognize these mental and emotional tensions as soon as they appear and take control over control by labeling them as childhood conditioning.

The ego's need to attract attention and be loved, results in tension, loneliness and long-term suffering. When you find yourself suffering from these kinds of thoughts, remember that there is no sustainable strategy to receive love. It all comes down to this: Love others. You get as much love as you give. There's no more than this.

Also remember that it is exhausting and unfeasible to try to receive through others the love that you do not give yourself. Be true to yourself and follow your heart. From that place everything will flow, and those who resonate with you will come into and nourish your life. Recognize, that loving and serving others, is one of the main sources of happiness that exists.

Identify your own thinking categories

Surely too, you can add other categories of thoughts, those which you discover reoccurring in your own mind. By learning to identify the types of thoughts you are having, as soon as they appear, and detaching from them, and by not giving them more energy, you will remove contractions from the mind and widen the space for an experience of awareness, the silent Presence, the unconditional joy of Being. You begin to do whatever comes your way to do, without feeling ruffled. You are generally happy.

● Practice: Knowing your habitual thoughts ●

Make a list by categories of thoughts that you usually cultivate. Observe how these thoughts repeat themselves throughout the day.

Consider what it would be like to be free from them.

Learn to identify them as soon as they appear again. Don't fight them, you just label them and don't give them more energy - like someone calling on the phone and you don't answer.

1- Neelakantan, V.T.N., Ramaiah, S.A.A. and Nagaraj, Babaji. (2003). *The Voice of Babaji; a trilogy of Kriya Yoga*. St. Etienne de Bolton, Quebec: Babaji's Kriya Yoga and Publications. p. 451.

The joy without object: the bliss of Self

Yoga is not an escape from everything, but a search of the heart of everything, of the Truth. The Siddhas did not confuse that Truth with emotions, thoughts or physical perceptions, and which are always changing. Nor did they consider the ego, the ordinary self, as something reliable, always in search of fruitless recognition or affection, and whose well-being is conditioned and deformed by subconscious patterns. So, the Siddhas had to look beyond. To look for a stable center is not to flee from an unstable world it is to look for the center of the wheel that turns. They found that center in pure consciousness, free from identification with everything that changes, and prescribed yogic practices to get there. Authentic, Yoga cannot be escapism - another mental pattern - but confrontation of all phenomena from that center of consciousness.

The Garden of Eden is inside us. When we become entangled in the pleasure and pain of the sensory experience we eat "the forbidden fruit of the tree of knowledge of good and evil" (Genesis 2:17), and we are expelled from the paradise of unconditional joy of Self, which is beyond the external dualities. We lose our Self in the search for objects. This is poetically expressed in the Bible in the story of Esau, who sold his right as firstborn (his filiation with the Self) for a plate of lentils (Genesis 25:27-34).

Ordinarily we ignore the difference joy, which is unconditional, and happiness, which depends upon getting what we desire or avoiding what we don't want. The mind attributes happiness with a condition or an object of experience, from the most elementary ones (food, body sensation, health) to the most subtle, including God. Happiness can be attributed to the experience of objects that we already have, or which we desire to experience in the future.

We can spend all our time of our life looking for happiness

chasing objects. Even in the spiritual quest we may chase experiences, objects or goals while forgetting our Self.

Self-inquiry is a path to the realization of Self. It is different from the path of Bhakti Yoga, seeking God as a personal being separated from oneself. In a way, devotional practice involves maintaining a subject-object duality, which may ultimately be transcended in the union of both through devotion and love. In self-inquiry we forget the object, whatever it is, and we focus on the subject.

Seeking the Subject, not the object

Consciousness is the most precious thing we have. It is not something outside of us, it is what we really are. Objects are manifested on the field of consciousness. With the practice of being the unconditional Witness we keep our consciousness safe from being absorbed by the phenomena we experience, inside and outside of us. We experience the unconditional joy of Self, which does not depend on circumstances. The Siddhas defined the Self as Existence-Consciousness-Joy; these three elements are inseparable.

We are That. Everything goes well until an object appears in our consciousness that arouses our aversion, such as fear or anger, or our desire, and then we are dragged to the life of dualities, and emotions arise. And we lose sight of our Self and our joy.

When the spirit is covered with this mortal nature, it begins to be affected by the continuous changes of the state of nature, and when it falls under the bond of attachment to changing things it is condemned to suffer in the endless cycle of reincarnations, according with his good or bad karma.

But the Supreme Spirit of man remains intact beyond his fate, he is a mere observer, he perceives everything, he suffers everything, he gives inspiration: he is known as the supreme Supreme Lord of the soul.

- Bhagavad Gita XIII.21-22

As you develop the witness consciousness and go beyond the mind and emotions, you discover the joy of Self, which is unconditional. This is true: it is there, without even the slightest doubt, regardless of what you believe. Even your doubts appear and disappear in it. You may become aware of what is aware when you silence the waves of thoughts and beliefs. And you discover that all Nature participates in that silent joy! Unconditional joy appears in each phenomenon, the same joy which is in the rain, in the flowering plants or in the passing clouds.

Yoga is universal. It does not limited by any system of beliefs. It addresses itself to the causes of human suffering, its misidentification. The internal inquiry, the practice of consciousness reveals the Truth within you: that free and joyful space in which you no longer need more questions and in which you would like to live forever.

The kingdom of heaven is like a treasure buried in a field, which a person finds and hides again, and out of joy goes and sells all that he has and buys that field.

– Matthew 13.44.

The joyful consciousness is buried below the level of vital experience of the person, like a treasure waiting to be discovered. When the yogi sells everything he has, that is, abandons all identifications and attachments, he can access it and enjoy it.

The yogi cultivates with care, patience and dedication his own consciousness, his most precious treasure. The joy that objects provide can be very intense, but it is never lasting; like the two sides of a coin, every pleasure has its opposite suffering. This temporary joy belongs to the emotional body. The joy of the subject, the unconditional bliss of Self, does not depend on anything except our attention, and is always there. And it belongs to our real and timeless nature, distinct from the changing world.

"Tantra" means "weave." Consciousness is the thread that interweaves all our experiences. Kriya means "action with awareness." Bringing unconditional awareness to ordinary life, the consciousness of the Witness, allows you to discover the space of pure being in everything: everything ends up woven into the consciousness and bliss of the Self. The Kriya Yoga of 18 Siddhas is the jewel of the tantric tradition.

I seat Myself in the very heart of delusion undeluded, I am ever steady and steadfast in all its tumblings and stumblings. I am always firm in all its fleetings.

- Kriya Babaji.[1]

In moments of dispersion or confusion remember that the treasure you seek is in you, in the blissful, pure and unconditioned consciousness. It is right there, in the very heart of delusion.

1- *The Voice of Babaji,* p. 233.

The consecration to the Satguru

Illuminating it is, to perceive guru's sacred person;
Illuminating it is, to chant guru's sacred name;
Illuminating it is, to listen to guru's sacred word;
Illuminating it is, to reflect on the guru's person.
- Tirumandiram, 139

Nandi's sacred feet, I am conjoined with;
Nandi's sacred person, I ponder over;
Nandi's sacred name, I chant;
Nandi's golden teaching remains in my mind.

- Tirumandiram, 141

The Siddhas are actually the worshipers of their guru. This fact distinguishes the followers of the Tantric faith from the followers of the Vedic faith who are called devabhaju or the worshippers of the devas. To the Siddhas the guru is invisible to the physical eye. The guru is also referred to as sunya (vastness of space or vettaveli) to indicate the spaciousness of freedom (or knowledge) in which the disciple loses himself.[1]

Attunement with the Satguru is also part of the beginning, the method and the goal of Kriya Yoga. The techniques of Kriya are nothing but a cleaning and preparation for this attunement which culminates in total surrender. "*God, guru and the Self itself are One,*" say the Siddhas. They praise surrender as the most important requirement for the transformation of the sadhaka into the divine.

"*Yogiar S.A.A. Ramaiah frequently reminded his innermost circle of disciples at the time that the greatest goal in Babaji's grand lineage was complete unconditional surrender to the Sathguru. Surrender to divine will, it seems, plays an important role in achieving the highest meditative states"* quotes Swami Ayyapa Giri, disciple of Yogi Ramaiah[2]. **This surrender is articulated in the sadhana, as the sadhaka identifies and releases internal contents**, samskaras and tendencies, thus leaving a free space that can be filled with the energy and grace of the Satguru. *"You cannot succeed unless you yourself exert and die"*; *"Self dying and making your own mansion, under God and Guru's grace are indispensable"* said Kriya Babaji.[3]

Devotees and disciples

A devotee and a disciple are different. The realized masters accept the devotion of the whole world and respond to it with a blessing or with grace - to the extent made possible by the karma of the devotee or by his receptivity. The devotee asks the teacher to help him with certain problems, and he can receive that help. Many people are in the level of devotees, in search of grace or help in obtaining limited purposes.

Being a disciple is something else. A disciple or sadhak is one who has made a sincere commitment to practice the disciplines or sadhana prescribed by the spiritual teacher. The disciple, rather than seeking favors for his life, surrenders all preferences to the adherence to this discipline, with confidence in the spiritual teacher, who then becomes responsible for the final realization of the disciple. He learns to receive the master's guidance through his internal attunement. The surrender of the disciple will ultimately include the surrender of his ego's perspective to the perspective of the Soul, the Self, the Witness. The disciple has realized the futility of trying to get rid of the ego with the limited means accessible to the ego, unaided by the spiritual teacher. Attempting Self-realization by yourself is like pretending to get yourself up off the ground by pulling yourself up; it is not possible, you need grip something above and beyond yourself in order to rise. One is only a disciple if a master accepts him, and the process of transformation of the student usually begins with the search for such acceptance.

Blissful attunement

The bodily form of a Satguru like Babaji is not important, although everyone wants to s his physical presence. Babaji is a state of consciousness, the personification of pure and loving consciousness, of timeless joy. A Satguru gives away freely his consciousness the more the disciple attunes inside with him. This is the true "communion" of which Jesus spoke and that true gurus emphasize, and not physical worship. A Satguru does not need our worship, but our constant attunement, in order to transmit his transforming energy and grace. However, you won't be able to attune in too much if you don't first make room inside and empty what now occupies your heart, including desires, fears and so on. The same thing that prevents you from fully tuning in with Babaji is what prevents you from seeing your Self. *"When you know who you are you will know who Babaji is"* said Yogi Ramaiah.

To enjoy Babaji's joy (*ananda*), one must first establish an inner attunement with him, turning away from external distractions and habitual tendencies. From this attunement and this surrender arises the ananda. It is a very specific bliss, which requires patient surrender, at the moment, without conditioned expectations about the results. This blissful attunement also provides guidance and inspiration for life.

The obstacle that stands between you and Babaji is the ego itself, with its baggage of inalienable emotional pleasures. This ego does not conceive the existence of ananda, the bliss of Self; it believes that life would be depressing by giving up on them. The sadhaka must learn to jump from pleasure, always dual with its corresponding suffering, to bliss, which is not dual, because it is the very nature of Self.

The Satguru guides, protects and directs the sadhaka on his

way to the complete realization of the Divine. The attunement of the sadhaka with the Satguru allows him to become receptive to his vibration, which implies a *shakti* of renewing grace. The sadhaka constantly keeps that attunement, and with the grace of the Satguru, confronts everything that happens, no matter what. *"'Catch God and Guru, never to leave, come what may, is the highest secret to success,' Kriya Babaji gives."* [4]

With time the sadhaka enters in the vibration of the Satguru through the constant repetition of his mantras and with the practice of the seventh meditation technique of Kriya Yoga, *Babaji Samyama Kriya.* You can get to feel the vibration of the attunement, and you also can feel when you lose it, but through yogic practices you can recover the connection with this vibration. The Satguru is always available and close, you just have to turn to him. With time and with sadhana this intuitive connection develops further. And with the advanced practices of Kriya Yoga the sadhaka develops attunement with the Satguru in the experience of the upper chakras: as light, as Aum or cosmic sound, as awareness of the One in everything.

A guide for our life lessons

Nature is designed to bring to us the lessons each of us needs to learn. Kriya, action with awareness is the vehicle and the destination. The Satguru is always there to guide us when we turn inwards toward Him as we seek to master the lessons that our soul confronts as it evolve. That is why it is essential to maintain contact and attunement with the Satguru to understand the teachings of these lessons and move forward, without getting stuck in our learning.

Moreover, the sadhaka may have his own ideas about what he needs to advance spiritually, and they may not correspond to what he really needs to learn to grow. Life will then direct its learning not to where the sadhaka wants, but where he needs to go to grow. And then the sadhaka may ask: "why I am here, if I am a spiritual person?" A good attunement with the Satguru, with his guidance and inspiration, will provide the understanding and help needed to focus the sadhak's energies in the right direction.

With time, the surrendered sadhaka discovers that the Satguru not only directs his sadhana but also the process of his life.

Surrender everything unto Babaji. Place your ego at His Lotus Feet and be at ease. He will take complete charge of you and your "unwanted baggage."Let him mold you anyway he likes. Let him do exactly as he wills. He will remove all defects and weakness.

– The Voice of Babaji[5]

Our progressive surrender to the Satguru and his learnings gradually eliminates our need to control everything in our lives - a useless effort from our part, because we cannot really control much, given our habits, tendencies, karma and delusion. The more we remove the manifestations of the ego, the more internal energy we release from the need to maintain its limited perspective.

The attunement with the Satguru is a source of inspiration and guidance; later it also becomes a powerful source of joy, and in advanced states it becomes a source of realization of the Self. Surrender to Satguru has to germinate in the emergence of Satguru within you, as your own real Self.

It is thus clear that the disciple meets his Satguru Deva *by the grace of God, whice he has deserved by his devotion to God in previous incarnations. Having thus met the* Satguru Deva, *he must now make further progress towards his goal by practicing devotion to* Satguru Deva *as God Incarnate. (...) it naturally follows that the* Satguru *is the Dweller in the Heart, both as God and the real Self. And from this fact, it also follows that to meditate on the* Satguru *as the real Self, is the means of activating the latent powers of the real Self by which deliverance is achieved.*

- The Voice of Babaji[6]

The Satguru, especially on the path of the Siddhas, is but the personal aspect of the Divine. Krishna points out in the Bhagavad Gita that the realization of the Self is easier with the personal aspect of the divine than with the impersonal aspect:

- Arjuna: Who are more versed in Yoga, the devotees who consistently worship you in this way or those who worship the Undying and Unmanifested?

- Krishna: Work is greater for those who put their mind on the Unmanifested, because the goal - the Unmanifested - is very difficult for humans to reach.

- Bhagavad Gita, XII, verses 1 and 5.

This personal relationship is a source of joy for the sadhaka and does not need the experience of the yogic samadhi. However, it complements perfectly well with the practice of samadhi. The accomplished yogi thus experiences the two sides of the Divine: the personal God (the Satguru) and the omnipresent impersonal God of samadhi.

Karma Yoga – surrender of karma or action

We spend most of our time working. We can turn that time into a yogic practice by offering the fruit of our work to the guru or the Divine. This is known as karma yoga. Karma yoga is not limited to any type of work but only to the degree of consciousness present during it. The practice of Yoga in all its forms expands our consciousness, unlike the ego, which contracts it. . The constant offering o dedication of actions to the Divine transforms ordinary action or our work into karma yoga. There are four affirmations inspired by the Bhagavad Gita that can be repeated as reminders of what surrender is:

- Everything belongs (I surrender) to the Dive.

- The Divine is in everyone, as the inner being.

- I free myself by following the will of Divine.

- The joy that I am really looking for is the divine joy.

These four statements can be useful to the devotee as a reminder of the surrender everything to the Higher Self - a process that is actually the only real option we have – to release the bonds on the ascending path to the One.

Another statement to repeat frequently at all times would be: "I completely surrender my past, my present and my future; I am free from everything in the Divine Satguru."

Real surrender to the Satguru occurs when everything that happens is offered to him and his guidance in the heart is followed.

When the devotee has surrendered unreservedly to the Divine, he is prepared to be able to launch himself without reservation to samadhi, the dissolution of the small "I" in the Absolute Consciousness.

Releasing personal baggage

We all experience karma, the consequences of thoughts, words and actions. Those which are experienced in the present life are known as "*prarabdha karma*." This karma includes events and conditions that we must experience and which are exhausted in this life. As we advance on the path towards our realization of the Self, we must face and resolve this prarabdha karma. Our sadhana must include a process of gradual exhaustion of this karma that manifests in our personal tendencies, without creating new karmas, known as "*asmita karma*".. To ignore this fact is to deceive oneself.

Mystics such as Saint John of the Cross or Thomas Merton spoke of three ways on the path to union with God: the purgative way, the illuminative way and the unitive way.

The Purgative Way, as the name implies, is that part of the long path which one treads towards the Godhead in which one purges oneself of all desires and attachments, of all imperfections, acts of commission and omission, shortcomings in renunciation and shortcomings in the total love of God, in the passion for the apprehension of the Godhead. The Illuminative Way is that part of the path which comes after the Purgative Way and in which one gains illumination, knowledge, gnosis. There is an intellectual aspect and an emotional aspect to this Way. There is a strong outpouring of the grace of God on the pilgrim treading this part of the long road to the Godhead. Last is the Unitive Way, that part of the pathway in which the pilgrim marches on with buoyant and joyous steps, filled with hope and freed from doubt or misconception.[7]

Someone defined Yoga as a mystical asceticism. So in our search for the realization of the Self, of God, we must keep in mind that we must go through the purgative way of which the mystics spoke. **The patience and persistence of the sadhaka must be inexhaustible as he advances in this process of releasing personal burdens**, until one day he begins to glimpse the light of the Guru and the Self in the so-called unitive way.

You must have patience, my child. You must tire patience with patience. Remember, there is a time for everything and everything in its own time.

– Kriya Babaji.[8]

Dissolving the heart in the Satguru

"*Chitta*" is a yogic term with several meanings, one of them describes the "heart" or in more psychological terms, the subconscious mind. It is the reserve of samskaras or subconscious patterns and the source of habitual tendencies and negative behavior. Yoga seeks the cleansing of this subconscious mind. Traditionally it was the role of the guru to subject the disciple to discipline in order to achieve this goal.

Devotional devotion to the Satguru, meditating in him, keeping him always in mind and dissolving the mind and the heart in this devotion also produces this cleansing process of *chitta.*

Dissolving the heart, *chitta,* in the Satguru is a direct and fast path towards realization of the Divine for those who are able to jump into this surrender. The sadhaka is thus transmuted in the heart, and his samskaras can be transformed by the grace of Satguru.

The secret is "being melted."Your mind must reach the melting point and your heart the bolinig point. It is only one syllable of a prayer or only one name repetition with namaste (Kriya Babaji Namasté) that can secure the whole grace showering work. The main point is that name or syllable should come from a mind which is already melted and a heart that is already boiling. All other things are only preliminaries to bring up that 'boiling and melting point.'

- The Voice of Babaji [9]

● Practice: Meditation on the Satguru ●

Visualize that the Satguru, Babaji or whoever you consider to be your teacher, is sitting in the center of your heart - if you don't have an image you can visualize the Satguru as light. From there the Satguru radiates golden light, purifying your whole being and dissolving all the karma in your heart.

You surrender completely to the Satguru, surrendering everything, including expectations, concerns and fears about the future, the control of your life. You leave nothing there.

Notice how as you surrender more things, you leave more free space in yourself, which is now filled by the light and energy of the Satguru. Feel and allow Him to inspire and guide your actions.

1- Ganapathy, T. N. (2003). *The Yoga of Siddha Boganathar Vol. 1.* St. Etienne de Bolton, Québec: Babaji's Kriya Yoga and Publications. p. 25.

2- Ayyapa Giri, S. (2014). *Samadhi Secrets of the Himalayan Mahavatar*

Babaji. http://kalipath.com/?p=10.

3- *The Voice of Babaji*, p. 255.

4- Id., p. 276.

5- Id., p. 428-429.

6- Id., p. 157-158.

7- Vanmikanathan, G. (1976). *Pathway to God Trod by Saint Ramalingar.* Bombay: Bharatiya Vidya Bhavan. Available in http://www.vallalar.org/English/V000009431B. p.48.

8- *The Voice of Babaji*, p. 33.

9- Id., p. 281.

Kundalini, the Energy that unifies your being

The main challenge of our growth towards the realization of the Self, towards Unity, is our internal fragmentation. We have multiple aspects and tendencies antagonistic within ourselves, each one with their own interests. Unifying all these aspects in the purpose of surrender to the Higher Self, to the service of the Divine, is the essential requirement for the realization of the Self. The Mother, of Sri Aurobindo Ashram, explains well this challenge of surrender and consecration to the Divine:

For your being is full of innumerable tendencies at war with one another — almost different personalities, we may say. When one of them gives itself to the Divine, the others come up and refuse their allegiance. "We have not given ourselves," they cry, and start clamoring for their independence and expression. Then you bid them be quiet and show them the Truth. Patiently you have to go round your whole being, exploring each nook and corner, facing all those anarchic elements in you which are waiting for their psychological moment to come up. And it is only when you have made the entire round of your mental, vital and physical nature, persuaded everything to give itself to the Divine and thus achieved an absolute unified consecration that you put an end to your difficulties. [1]

Kundalini is the spiritual energy that is said to sleep in the first chakra, and that an intense yogic practice can cause her to awaken and rise through the spine, in search of union with Siva, in the crown chakra.

Upon awakening the divine energy of Kundalini brings to light all our different internal aspects, our tendencies, and threads them like the thread of the rosary that links all its beads. Everything that was hidden comes to light. All our tendencies are always there, from our oldest incarnations. Some are present in our consciousness, directly conditioning our behavior; others remain asleep at the bottom of our psyche, waiting for the right moment to germinate.

The habits of other lives want to come to light, pushed by kundalini, which infuses a lot of energy into the yogi's system, to make it move towards samadhi (union), and then all resistance to this advance also comes to light. By making these latent tendencies conscious you can stop holding them unconsciously, since they are still there in the psyche for the approval you gave them in other lives.

Kundalini is the power that completes creation, the way back of the energy to the One, which brings to light all the impediments for this realization. Kundalini is retained by the accumulated karma, which reveals itself as obstacles in its ascending path. This karma is what you put the energy into in the past. You put your intention in these obstacles to create them and now you put your attention back to them to free them. Consider these latent tendencies as something alien to you and now redirect your energy, without repressing it, towards its union with the crown chakra.

Kundalini, as power, leads you to the Self. That power seeks the Divine and helps you transmute your psyche. It is a manifestation of the Divine Mother, contemplate everything as Her action. She is helping you to grow, to leave the world of suffering, bringing to the surface your bonds to it. She takes you out of there. If you have patience and accept her dance, Kundalini will help you eliminate the stain of ignorance

In Yoga in general and in Kriya Yoga in particular, this awakening of Kundalini is not a sudden and definitive event. It is rather a gradual process: as the sadhaka advances in his yogic practice, this energy goes reaching and bringing to light new tendencies and contents, new dispersed "I's", which must be integrated into the student's consciousness. So, Kundalini is the great unifier of the psyche of the Yoga sadhaka; in the long term, she works for the expansion of the sadhak's consciousness, threading into it all of the sadhak's different aspects. However, this unification is but the end of a laborious process that will require inexhaustible perseverance, patience, serenity and dedication by the yogi. To finish this process you will need to be well equipped with tools and yogic qualities, in addition to having the protection of divine grace, personified in the figure of the guru.

Channeling the energy

As Kundalini gradually becomes activated the sadhak will find greater amounts of energy available. What to do with it? The sadhak must learn to channel it into activities of love and service, so that Kundalini continues to rise. Love is expansive. Egoism contracts energy. Without loving, selfless outlets, the Kundalini serpent will stop its ascent and feed the ego's manifestations such as desire, pride, fear, and anger, stopping the advance of the sadhak.

On the positive side, kundalini will also stimulate the qualities, abilities and positive tendencies of sadhaka such as creativity, charisma, intuition, kindness and discernment. This increase in abilities can ultimately lead to the development of *siddhis* - which is usually translated as "yogic powers." But they are part of the latent potential we all have.

The need of purifying the ego

Traditionally, on the path of Yoga in India, the disciple could be tested by his guru, to whom he rendered an unconditional service that served to purify his character and ego, before being fully accepted and receiving advanced teachings.

Milarepa underwent a series of struggles during his service to the Guru. *He had to perform superhuman acts of heroism and bravery before he was initiated. Sages and rishis of yester-years, put their students to severe trials before they took them into their confidence and divulged the mysteries of mysticism and occultism. They intuitively knew whether a student was ripe for initiation or not. The neophytes were entrusted with the work of tending cows, bringing fuel from the forest to the ashram, washing the clothes of the guru and offered work that would appear to be menial service in the eyes of present-day modern-metamorphosed* sadhakas.

- The Voice of Babaji[2]

Most of the current Yoga practitioners do not have such masters who may help with the purifying of disciples' egos. Therefore, the sadhak can use the opportunities and difficulties of life itself to apply the following However, when advancing on the path of Yoga the sadhaka must be prepared before executing advanced yogic techniques that involve the activation of the chakras or Kundalini energy. In Kriya Yoga it is advisable to be well established in certain fundamental practices and behaviors to round off the rough edges of the ego:

- Detachment, inner concentration and consciousness of the witness, which will prevent the student from being distracted and absorbed by what that emerges in the mind.

- Surrender to Satguru and to the path, to avoid being dispersed by multiple new stimuli that may arise as one advances. Surrender does not imply not to be mistaken, but the resolution to persist in practice no matter the obstacles that arise; and even if these obstacles are not overcome, the sadhaka continues on the path with the confidence that one day it will be possible to leave them behind.

- Habit of service to other beings. With an intense yogic practice the sadhak, available energy is multiplied. The question is what to do with this increased energy? Unconditional service to all beings, surrendering the results to the Divine (Karma Yoga) is the most dharmic, straight application of all this extra energy, and will often facilitate its integration. Service to all beings removes the ego of the sadhaka and reveals the nature of the Self, which unconditionally gives and serves all.

The management and integration of Kundalini fire is best understood if you ask yourself these questions: Currently, what do I spend my energy on, consciously and unconsciously? And what would happen to me then if this energy were multiplied by a thousand?

The process of managing Kundalini energy begins with the cultivation of Presence and Love - being aware of daily activities and discovering where the energy itself goes - and culminates in the unhindered expansion of Presence and Love. Between the beginning and the end there is a patient and tireless process of transmutation. Detachment, surrender and service will facilitate over and over again the advancement of sadhaka through the stony path of his transformation.

1- Mother, the. (2003). *Questions and Answers 1929-1931*. Pondicherry: Sri Aurobindo Ashram Publications Department. p. 127.

2- *The Voice of Babaji*, p.364.

Kundalini and the liberation of inner tendencies

They tell a story in India that the gods and the demons agreed to churn the cosmic ocean to obtain the *amrita*, the nectar of immortality. But in doing so, the first thing that emerged was the poison, a terrible poison that could kill everyone. Everyone fled from it. Only Shiva, beyond all duality, agreed to take that poison, to protect the creation. He swallowed it, but the poison stopped in his throat, did not reach his stomach. As a result his throat turned blue. That is why one of the names of Shiva is Nilakantan, which means "blue throat".

The intense practice of pranayams (churning of the cosmic ocean) as *Kriya Kundalini Pranayama* brings to the surface the *samskaras* - all kinds of habitual patterns lodged in the subconscious mind. The yogi must be well settled in the detachment to handle these patterns, which mean accepting them but not absorbing them – just as Shiva swallowed the poison, but did not absorb or identify with it.

There is a somewhat romantic conception that Kundalini energy awakens within the sadhak, rises directly and automatically to the crown chakra, and the yogi gets forever enlightened. But in reality that would be only the end of a long process of transformation, and it would only be possible when the internal energy circuit formed by the chakras and nadis is purified and activated.

Until that time comes, Kundalini raises increasingly the level of consciousness - through the practice of *Kriya Kundalini Pranayama*, Kriya Hatha Yoga, Kriya Dhyana Yoga and Kriya Mantra Yoga. This means that what was hitherto unconscious becomes conscious, and a process of purification begins to unleash. And the advanced Yoga student must be well prepared to face it.

The Apocalypse arrives

The Christian book of the Apocalypse of St. John tells how after the opening of seven seals and the touch of seven trumpets, a great cosmic commotion takes place, the heavens are polarized between good and evil. The dead come back to life and a selection is done, they bring the resurrected good ones to the eternal life and the wicked ones to the eternal damnation.

Reading this text of St. John from a yogic perspective reveals interesting meanings. The opening of the chakras, the seven seals or the seven trumpets, can activate and bring to consciousness a lot of material associated with each one of them, memories and samskaras, something that can be certainly overwhelming. Then we need to put discernment, as the celestial forces - our higher tendencies – do, and separate those samskaras that make us advance (the good ones) and let go and dissolve those that divert us (the evil ones) from our spiritual path. A small Final Judgment that we must incorporate into our daily yogic practice, with awareness, calm and detachment.

Kundalini releases everything

As Kundalini is activated this process of liberation of samskaras is also precipitated. The yogi must neither suppress nor encourage them. The yogi must learn to "let go" of them. This is the cultivation of vairagya, detachment.

Have you ever prepared ghee, clarified butter? You take a solid stick of butter and put it to simmer in a saucepan. After a while, the butter turns into a golden liquid, but lumps and impurities appear, and you must remove from the liquid while it continues to boil. Before, you had no problems, you had a seemingly homogenous and solid block, and now, to get the golden and crystalline ghee, you have to eliminate a lot of impurities that were not seen at the beginning.

The fire of kundalini acts in a similar way as it gets more intense. It polarizes what once seemed a homogeneous psyche, drawing impurities to the light, while purifies our consciousness. Kundalini aspires to unite with the crown chakra, and in its ascent it will not leave anything behind; it will bite any tendency or impurity that it finds within its reach.

Those tendencies that were stored in the depths of our psyche and that Kundalini brings to consciousness seek their own fulfillment, and are the seeds that will cause future reincarnations. They are long-held desires, and also obstacles such as fears, resentments, sadness, despair... negativities all stored since many lives back.

Kundalini cleans slowly but completely, and over time it will release all these seeds that hinder our progress, one after the other, until only pure consciousness remains. And this is where the internal battle mentioned metaphorically in the Bhagavad Gita begins. There is narrated how the warrior Arjuna faints when he realizes that, by chance, he will have to fight against his relatives and old friends. Arjuna is the yogi who understands that he will have to face his own tendencies, so dear to him, as they separate him from the path to the Divine. But then Krishna, the voice of the Divine, encourages him to do so: "*Thus, O Arjuna, destroy with the sword of knowledge the doubts that arise from the ignorance that dwells in your heart. Through Yoga, become one with this harmony that is inside you. Get up, great warrior, get up* "- Bhagavad Gita 42.IV. And he reminds him that no effort in Yoga, no matter how small, will be in vain.

Yogic tools

As a result of the above, I would also suggest the following yogic tools to release the emerging samskaras and to continue our yogic path:

- The frequent use of a notebook as a spiritual diary to understand our internal processes and to note and let go conflicting thoughts and emotions, writing them to objectify them and then letting them go.

- Be present and aware in the moment. The samskaras are the filters of the past that want to color the present moment and condition the future. By being fully present we can see them consciously and let them leave at the moment they appear. Actually, the only thing we have is the present moment. The mind and the samskaras intend to reinterpret reality as a continuous past and future, but neither the past nor the future are real, they do not exist: they are only mental projections. There is only the present.

- Meditation of detachment - it is especially interesting to practice it at night, before sleeping, because it is a time when the subconscious and its contents emerge, an opportune moment when they can be released. Furthermore, after this meditation we may enter sleep with the awareness of detachment and continue the process of purification of the subconscious. Mataji, the spiritual shakti of Babaji, can be invoked to help us in the nightly cleansing process of samskaras - she is a master of Shuddi Dhyana, the meditation of detachment. The sincere invocation of grace can produce unexpected help.

- Work with the chakras (see next chapters). There is a series of samskaras associated with each chakra and the yogic practice releases them, which includes material from previous lives. The chakras are rooted in the psyche and in the subconscious, so by purifying the chakras we also purify our mind, liberating consciousness.

The poems of the Siddhas propose meditations with different chakras, associating them with certain deities and mantras. In Kriya Yoga (third level) we invoke Babaji in the work with the chakras. Working one chakra per day, trying to tune it with Babaji, helps its activation / purification. For this we have various tools, such as *Mandira Matreika Pranayama* and the dhyanas of the chakras, which include the mantra and the asana.

- The repetition of positive affirmations allows us to counteract the samskaras of negative tendencies. Repeating them during the Yoga Nidra practice helps us to install them without resistance in the subconscious mind.

- Clear the seeds of the samskaras by repeatedly entering the state of deep meditation or samadhi.

- As always, in first and last place, invoke Grace from the heart, through chanting, prayesr, the devotional repetition of the mantras - among which I would highlight the *Durga* and *Muruga* mantras, the *complete surrender to Babaji* mantra and the mantras of *Mataji* and the Siddhas. Grace always exceeds our efforts, so invoking it and becoming receptive to it will make it much more effective on us. Ultimately, the sadhana of Kriya Yoga is nothing but a cleansing of our bodies to become solid vessels of the divine Grace.

The advanced practice of activating the chakras

Lord Muruga: a transmutation of consciousness

"When you worship Lord Krishna you get Krishna consciousness, when you worship Muruga or Kartikeya you get Kartikeya consciousness, in which the six chakras are awakened. In Kartikeya you find six faces, corresponding with the six chakras, the seventh is hidden inside. So the six faces of Kartikeya indicate that the six chakras have been awakened. That is exactly the significance of Kartikey".[1]

- Yogi Ramaiah

Kartikeya or Muruga, the son of Shiva, is a much adored deity in South India. At the beginning of the Kali Yuga, the Siddha Boganathar himself dedicated to Muruga the temples of Palani, in Tamil Nadu, and Katirgama, in Sri Lanka as a means for devotees to progress spiritually. The image of Lord Muruga, like most Hindu symbolism, transmits teachings at different levels of understanding, including those related to the path of the Siddhas.

Another of Muruga's names is Skanda, which means "do not spill." T.N. Ganapathy writes about it in his book "The philosophy of the Tamil Siddhas":

Skanda is born only when the semen is sublimated and reaches the sahasrar. Lord Muruga is said to reside only on mountain tops (i.e., sahasrara region). Ascending the mountain to reach Lord Muruga is a symbolism for arousing the kundalini and its culmination in saharara. The six adharas (chakras) are considered to be the six mountains in Tamil Siddha literature, and the six faces of Lord Muruga stand for them.[2]

Muruga is represented as a boy, sometimes a teenager. Like the archangel St. Michael in Christianity, he is said to be in

charge of the army of the heavenly forces. He has a spear called Vel, with which he fights the darkness. According to the legend it was Parvati, the Divine Shakti, his Mother, who gave him that spear to facilitate his task of fighting against the negative forces. With it Muruga defeated a demon that threatened the world, but he did not destroy him, but transformed him into a peacock, which since then happened to be his mount. In the images of Muruga this peacock often appears dominating a snake. A rooster - the animal that announces the light of dawn - also appears on the banner of Muruga.

The spear of Muruga represents the transmutation of sexual and vital energy into spiritual energy, and also the awakening of kundalini energy. **This transmutation is a fundamental feature of the path of the Siddhas**, and is also represented by the image of the peacock dominating the serpent - the demon that was not destroyed but transmuted into the mount of Muruga. The texts of the Siddhas speak of the transmutation of *bindu* (semen, vital energy) into *ojas* (spiritual energy).

By raising the vital energy from the chakras or lower psychoenergetic centers to the higher centers, light arises in them, symbolized by the rooster announcing the light of the new day. This energy reverts not only at the physical level, but at the vital level also, and then to the mental level, elevating and spiritualizing these bodies.

Muruga, who originally had six faces, fights the demons in six mountains, the six chakras (the seventh chakra, *sahasrara*, is not considered a chakra but the abode of the Self). Vel, the spear of Muruga, also represents the discernment, the awakened witness consciousness, empowered by the transmutation of vital energy, which brings the light of consciousness to the mountains of the six chakras.

According to legends Muruga was born from the light of Shiva's third eye, and after growing up he descended from Mount Kailash in Tibet to Mount Palani, in Tamil Nadu, where he settled and married a girl from a local tribe. In Muruga we also have the archetype of the descent of grace from superior to inferior chakras, to transform them. The legends say that the seed of Shiva that shaped Muruga was scorching and difficult to contain. This makes us think of the supramental consciousness of which Sri Aurobindo spoke, whose descent can transform even the physical body. A consciousness too powerful to be tolerated by the ordinary man, which requires a complete transformation and surrender on the part of the sadhaka.

Regarding our sadhana, Muruga teaches us the importance of transmuting sexual and vital energy into spiritual energy as a basic tool of transformation. Taoism and the writings of Siddha Boganathar insist a lot on this idea. This transmutation, if done correctly, is the key to opening the upper chakras. It also produces an expansion of consciousness that allows us to detect and release the samskaras or inner patterns of behavior. The transmutation of our energy also releases the light in our inner space, and finally the invocation of the descent of the Divine and of his Grace in this light opens the path of the sadhaka towards a transformation in the Divine of its subtle and dense bodies - the goal of the Siddhas.

1- Ramaiah, S.A.A. (2019). *Babaji's Kriya Yoga Lectures of Yogi S.A.A. Ramaiah.*
https://babajiskriyayogalecturesofyogisaaramaiah.simplecast.fm/13c0f6f1
2- Ganapathy, T.N. (1993). *The philosophy of the Tamil Siddhas.* New Delhi: Indian Council of Philosophical Research. p. 23.

The sadhana of the chakras

The centres of consciousness, the chakras. It is by their opening that the Yogic or inner consciousness develops — otherwise you are bound to the ordinary outer consciousness. The more they open, the more the consciousness increases.

– Sri Aurobindo[1]

When the six flowers are blossomed, the six chakras become the shrine of God. Try to worship God in the six shrines inside. You should do intense sadhana and allow Babaji to descend to these chakras.

– Yogi Ramaiah[2]

Whether you activate and elevate the kundalini energy or if the divine Grace descends from higher planes, you must prepare yourself for it: your physical, vital, mental bodies are the vessels that must be capable of receiving and containing that higher Grace and energy.

The chakras, centers of consciousness and energy distributed throughout our column, are the mediators between heaven and earth. They take root in the subconscious, in the deepest mind, but if they are activated and become divine, they divinize everything. The Kriya Yoga of the Siddhas is the sadhana of building a living space for the Divine in us and filling it with Its light. That is why the divinization of the chakras is emphasized. Other yogic schools use them as rungs in the ascending stairs to higher planes, in search of liberation and the end of the rebirths in this physical world

In our psyche there are karmic traces or tendencies called "samskaras," which frequently activate unwanted, sometimes automatic, responses in the emotional and mental bodies. When a person gets carried away by these unwanted answers, instead of confronting them from the witness, he ends up feeling bad. These responses create an environment in the psyche that constitutes the "personality" of the ordinary individual, who usually lives as a reaction to these responses.

In the Yoga of the Siddhas our consciousness is also expanded in the seven chakras. Each chakra has conscious and unconscious samskaras related to each of tit. Negative samskaras, those that prevent us from growing and manifesting our divine potential, must be revealed, released and overcome so that they become ineffective and stop activating unwanted responses. As one advances in Yoga, the sadhak becomes more aware of these dissonant responses that come from these karmic traces. The energetic-mental structure that sustains the ego is formed by all these samskaras. This structure must be replaced by the structure of the Self, formed by the activated chakras, vibrating in tune with Kriya Babaji, our Higher Self.

Purifying, tuning and activating the chakras

The chakras have to be threaded to vibrate together. All the diverse practices to activate them are fine, including advanced meditations on them. In these the student tries to put his consciousness in each of them, to integrate and activate them.

This work can be tedious, but it is adequate and necessary. Sometimes consciousness "leaves" when meditating on them.

The sadhaka must go beyond the pleasant or the unpleasant, as experienced in the vital body. By intense and sustained concentration, the sadhak penetrates the mental and vital bodies and accesses the potential power and consciousness beyond them. Strengthening the witness beyond the vital body brings the emergence of *ananda*; the unconditional joy of the Self emerges more and more in the life of the sadhaka.

To perform an intense sadhana in the chakras it is required to be solidly installed in the Heart Witness and to have developed the ability to let go all kinds of emotions.

The attempt to activate a chakra can release deeply the contents related to it: memories, limiting or pessimistic thoughts, conflicting emotions, negative tendencies, or the emotional nuclei mentioned in the chapter "Bringing the Heart Witness to the emotional body." These contents emerge in droves and you don't have to follow them, just release them by letting them go. Accept that they are there, take them and release them.

These karmic traces that are activated by the practice of Yoga arise in consciousness for its manifestation or its final eradication. They are like seeds that are looking for the moment to germinate. When this happens, they come to light, and then they can be eradicated from their roots. So, the emergence of these contents, if properly focused, is an unusual opportunity for growth and advancement.

The consciousness of the sadhaka must, on the one hand, become sufficiently plastic to allow these contents to emerge, without suppressing them and without judging them, without guilt, without even interest. When they emerge and they are suppressed, anxiety, discomfort or fear may generated. And, on the other hand, the consciousness of the sadhaka must know that it can accept them - because they have emerged as spoiled tendencies cultivated in previous lives. After recognizing them, the sadhaka can release them and let them go, declaring that "I am not going to put more energy here anymore, because I'm not interested in this anymore." **It is a process of feeling, accepting, integrating and releasing.**

Karmic seeds sink into the subconscious mind, and their origins date back to the beginning of the incarnations. They say in India that there is no saint without a past or sinner without a future. Everyone has gone through all kinds of experiences throughout innumerable incarnations, which have left their trail at the bottom of our psyche. So, the realized yogis have previously eradicated all kinds of samskaras. One is not one´s own samskaras, which are the fruit of the chance of *samsara*, the endless wheel of reincarnations. One is the blissful witness, and the more one releases the samskaras, the freer one´s conditioning remains.

The student must find the appropriate frequency and intensity to perform this sadhana of the chakras, since the eruption of their deeply held contents can be disturbing, and then it takes time for these contents to be integrated into the consciousness. It is important to find a rhythm of sadhana that the student can follow, without being overwhelmed by them. If the sadhana is performed at night, the activation of the contents of the chakras can prevent you from falling sleep. Having previously done a lot of Shuddi practice, the meditation of detachment, creates a good basis for undertaking this sadhana of the chakras. It is very useful to use a notebook to write and let go the samskaras that are released, which may include experiences and tendencies from previous lives.

It is also important to work on all the chakras to achieve a balanced development.

After the liberation of these dense contents there is an expanding space of light and peace, and the sadhak advances considerably towards the unconditional freedom of the Self.

● **Practice: Activation of the chakras** ●

Focus on each one of the chakras, ascending from bottom to top:

- Muladhara or root center in the perineum.

- Swadhistana in the sacrum.

- Manipura in the solar plexus.

- Anahata in the heart.

- Visuddhi in the throat.

- Ajna on the forehead.

- Sahasrara in the crown.

As you focus on them you repeat the Om Kriya Babaji Nama Aum mantra on each one. Do it without rushing. First you focus on the chakra, you notice its energy. Then you repeat the mantra making it vibrate in the chakra, and notice how its energy changes. Feel that the vibration of the mantra cleanses its impurities and activates it, so that it begins to radiate light.

After reaching the crown, you visualize the seven chakras giving off golden light, aligned in the light of the Satguru.

1- Doshi, N. (1974). *Guidance from Sri Aurobindo, Letters to a Young Disciple. Volume 1*. Auroville: Sri Aurobindo Ashram Trust. p. 8.

2- Ramaiah, S.A.A. (2019). *Tamil Kriya Yoga Siddhantham – Homes*. Available in:
    https://babajiskriyayogalecturesofyogisaaramaiah.simplecast.fm/13c0f6f1

The lower chakras and sensuality

When the time comes, you will have to walk through fire and water.

- Haidakhan Baba[1]

The activation of the lower chakras can increase desires and the appetite for the enjoyment of sensual experiences, in all their forms and aspects. An appetite that seems to have no limit or end.

The wise have confirmed that the test of purification of the navel chakra is the upsurge of an abundance of all the worldly desires. The desire for enjoyment of physical pleasures will become accentuated and increase. This state is the test of the churning of the navel chakra.

If, indeed, he has bridled the urge for the pleasures of the world, the cosmic energy awakened will grant him many spiritual powers.

- Sri Sadashiv Charitamrit, verses 374-375[2]

Regarding sexual energy, the daily practice of bandhas and pranayamas such as *Brahmacharya Ojas Matreika* facilitates their transmutation into spiritual energy, *ojas* (for those not initiated in Babaji Kriya Yoga in the appendices is included a breathing exercise to transmute sexual energy). In this way we eliminate much of the physical stimulation of sexual desire. As the energy rises, so does the consciousness. The fundamental principle of Tantra is that consciousness follows energy and energy follows consciousness.

The most important work of transmutation of sexual energy and mental dispersion on a physical, mental and emotional level is the control of the imagination. First, by practicing detachment from the mental images of desire as soon as they appear. We must treat these images as what they are, a deception of the uncontrolled mind. Desires, like fears, rarely correspond to reality. Second, we must also take care in the choice of sense objects, avoiding those that may activate our imagination or *vasanas*. *Vasanas* are tendencies to dwell on particular pleasant or unpleasant memories. When they do arise, one must be careful to neither encourage nor suppress them, but to calmly "let go" of them with firm detachment and disinterest.

Sri Aurobindo says regarding the role of imagination here:

To let the memory or imagination dwell on things that excite the sex-desire is unhealthy for the sadhana and an obstacle to the development of the Yogic consciousness. Discourage these imaginations and memories when they come. That [support of the sex-sensation by the imagination] is the difficulty. The imagination means a consent of the physical or else the vital mind. Otherwise the [sex-] sensation is often only due to physical causes and, if not supported by this automatic assent of a part of the mind, would before long diminish in its habit of recurrence.

Care must be taken that the sexual or erotic imagination does not take hold of the consciousness.[3]

We know all sensual pleasures are dual; they have their ups and downs, unlike the unconditional bliss of Self. And the physical body is finally consumed by these pleasures. We do not judge this enjoyment of desires from a moral point of view, but from the point of view of the yogi who wants to continue advancing on the path to supreme happiness. From this point of view, we don´t want that the energy awakened by yogic practice to become stagnant and amplified in the lower chakras, impeding drastically our personal evolution and our realization of the Self.

On the other hand, sexual energy should not be neglected, but transmuted: **the yogi preserves it and elevates it to the upper chakras, using its force to activate and open them**. This transmutation also has the effect of revitalizing the physical body.

In addition to this, the transmutation of sexual energy raises consciousness to a level where it can remain detached from fears and desires, rather than absorbed by them.. And to reach and maintain the states of samadhi the maximum amount of energy accessible by the sadhak is needed. Therefore, the sadhak must avoid the loss of seminal fluids or energy in both males and females during sexual intercourse.

Babaji stresses the importance of celibacy in Yoga sadhana, for one who pursues yogic methodology without loss of vital energy would be able to reap the benefits of realization of spiritual bliss to the fullest extent.

- The Voice of Babaji[4]

The paradox is that sometimes the activation of kundalini and the lower chakras stimulates sexual desire to extremes not experienced before. This is an incessant source of difficulties for the vast majority of advanced yogis: a hard test that all sadhaks must sometimes experience. In the Ramayana it is narrated how Ravana, one of the devotees of the god Shiva who attained yogic powers by his great penance, was destroyed along with his kingdom by his lustful desire for Sita, the consort of Rama, a divine incarnation. Hanuman, the celibate monkey god at the service of Rama, set the city of Ravana on fire with his tail, leaving it burning. Hanuman can be interpreted as the vital body transmuted to the service of the Divine, which abandons the attractions of the lower chakras. Hanuman was also the son of the wind (a reference to pranayama, which is cultivated in the vital body).

The Siddhas also use the practice of transmuting sexual energy with their partners, using the breath to draw it towards the upper chakras, taking care that there is no emission of seminal fluids by the male. The Tirumandiram of the Siddha Tirumular dedicates a section to this subject under the title of "Pariyanga Yoga", in its third *tantra* or chapter.

The lover and the beloved, performing the Yoga of love
Guide the chariot, moving in regions outer wings
Take it on the flow of heavenly waters

- Tirumandiram 827

To the yogin and his consort, grief there shall be none
The silvery liquid in the body will not downward flow, but
rise.

- Tirumandiram 837

Through yoga one copulates in a way to not waste bindu
Even when two bodies are united, bindu *will not be lost.*

- Tirumandiram 1960

Taoism adherents have similar practices. Both spiritual lineages, the lineage of the Siddhas of South India and Taoism, affirm that immortality is the ultimate attainment achieved by the masters of their paths.

As the energy of the lower chakras is transmuted, the sadhak grows in bliss and consciousness. If nothing is left in them, the sadhak no longer return there, neither now, nor in a future birth to fulfill its desires. The work of the transmutation is more definitive than it seems.

● **Practice: transmuting sexual energy** ●

This breath will help you to transmute the sexual energy into spiritual energy. You can practice it as often as you consider:

With the inhalation the sexual energy is drawn from the genitals to the crown at the top of the head, raising it as it is inhaled. On exhalation, this energy is rotated at the top of the head, clockwise, turning it nine times. Thus, this energy is concentrated at the top of the head. The process is repeated over and over again, without haste and with patience. After a while the practitioner may notice that this sexual energy has subsided, and one feels full of vitality.

This practice can be performed alone or with a partner, during sexual intercourse - the two practitioners coordinate their breaths, performing this practice at the same time. In this way, both transmute sexual energy together, avoiding the loss of sexual fluids and the consequent loss of energy. This practice also greatly reinforces the spiritual bond and the energy of the couple.

The seminal essence, *bindu*, is channeled and raised. In the upper chakras it is transmuted into spiritual energy that expands in the omnipresent Om. From the state of division, manifested in *bindu*, one goes to the All: one turns from multiplicity to Unity - the way of the Siddhas.

The sadhaka must emphasize this transmutation and then expand the light of the higher centers until it encompasses everything, including the physical.

1- Shri Haidakhan Babaji's Online Ashram. *The Teachings of Babaji 1979-1984*. p. 17. Available in:
https://www.truthsimplicitylove.com/
2- Mahendra Baba, Mahendra, Shastriji, Babaji. *Sri Sadashiv Charitamrit* (provisional translation).
3- Aurobindo, Sri. (2015). *Letters on Yoga IV*. Pondicherry: Sri Aurobindo Ashram Publications Department. p. 523-524.
4- *The Voice of Babaji*, p. 203.

The center of the solar plexus and the energy of fire

Manipura, the third chakra, provides the energy required to fulfill all desires beyond the base desires to procreate and survive associated with the first two chakras. It is the source of the willpower to achieve all desires. It corresponds to the fire element and the vital or emotional body. It is a center of fire, will and power. For what desire or purpose will spend the energy generated by your yogic practice in this center?

The vital body is the seat of desire and all emotions.

When desires are not realized, there can be frustration. If one ignores one's true identify, such frustration may give rise to hate and anger. Such passions can be profound obstacles to spiritual advancement. Hate is deeply rooted in the vision of duality. Considering something as different and opposite to you chains you. We humans like to take sides for on issues and fight against its opposite. That is the trap of the third chakra, falling into a duality and fighting eternally against the opposite..

Sometimes the test required to ascend from the consciousness of the third chakra to that of the fourth is to renounce the duality of liking and disliking, attachment and aversion, conditional love and hatred. We can see this duality in politics, in sports, in tribal wars, in nationalism ... hatred against the "other." This is mental delusion, *maya*; in reality there is no "other", only One, Divinity everywhere.

The opposite of dualistic thinking is to concentrate on That which transcends everything in time and space. This is the mystic perspective or vision of the One, of the only Divine reality in everything around us. So how can we hate, if the One is all that?

We hate an object out of ignorance of our unity with it and fear immediately springs forth with the duality. On the contrary, when we are at home with the whole world, manifesting our inner, divine love and love alone, we recognize that the one Reality without a second results.

- The Voice of Babaji[1]

Sooner or later the sadhaka must transcend this duality if he wants to move towards the experience of the One. This means raising the consciousness from the third to the fourth chakra, where unconditional love rules and brings the realization of Unity, and in which the neighbor is as yourself.

Can one experience samadhi, Oneness, while clinging to dualities? Impossible. As you move towards samadhi these past dualities could emerge into your consciousness, to be resolved: hatreds, unresolved conflicts, etc.

To get out of the trap dualistic thinking and its consequent suffering see the Divinity behind situations and people who bother us and create conflicts, and consider to what extent you may have created them out of your own tendencies and aversions. Forgive others and yourself, and let go of these tendencies.

Energetic transmutation of *agni*, the inner fire

Intense yogic practice stimulates the fire of kundalini, which can be felt especially in the fire of the plexus. **This energy must be accepted and transmuted, without rejecting it but without allowing it to be diverted towards thoughts or feelings of ambition, resentment, hatred or destruction (fire element)**. It is an energy that, like sexual energy, can feed our spiritual advancement. It must be carried to the heart, and converted into Presence and Love.

Just as we can transmute sexual energy into spiritual energy, we can also transmute *agni*, the fire of the solar plexus to the heart center as the expression of love. Many asanas, the practice of Bhakti Yoga (the Yoga of devotion), and especially the acts of unconditional service of Karma Yoga (the yoga of selfless action), are effective for this purpose.

Devotional chanting is very useful to transmute this fire; we project our love in the song and then send that loving energy to everyone.

The asanas and bandhas of Kriya Yoga create the basis of this transmutation. *Brahmacharya Ojas Maitreka Pranayama* and dog breathing (kriya # 66, *Nye Pranayama*) may also be useful. We can also energetically transmute this fire by consciously bringing it to the center of the chest, the heart center: when we inhale we draw it from the solar plexus to the fourth chakra, when we exhale we expand it there.

Avoiding dinner at night, if possible, or eating very little, may be helpful, since digestion stimulates low agni, and by fasting it can be transmuted, just as sexual energy can be transmuted rather than lost during sexual activities. Overeating reduces digestive fire. The physical dinner can thus be replaced by a spiritual feast of devotional activities.

It is also useful to avoid creating low *agni* energy with gossip, resentment, political animosity, violent movies and addictive behavior. Cultivate activities or entertainments that inspire higher values and love. Become fully aware of how you use your energy, how much of it is wasted, and the consequences of its use in terms of your habits and tendencies.

A successful transmuting the fire of *agni* from the third chakra into the unconditional love of the fourth chakra will be a turning point in your sadhana.

1- *The Voice of Babaji,* p. 232.

The center of the heart and Oneness through love

There comes a time when the sadhak no longer finds satisfaction in the fulfillment of sensory desires and experiences, and then becomes a seeker in what lies beyond. One seeks to escape the prison of egoism. The sincere seeker is eventually blessed with a spiritual experience which includes unconditional love. This occurs with an opening of the heart chakra. Before then, it's like going around in the same room, with no other way out. But now the terms are reversed: with the lower chakras you looked for getting things or experiences, but now, to continue to experience unconditional love you have to give. There is no logic here. But when the flower of the sadhak's chest begins to open, nothing else is worth pursuing. In the heart one realize the true Self.

The opening of the heart center is the key to the spiritual advancement of sadhak. This opening occurs to the extent that the sadhak feels an unconditional flow of love towards all beings. The fire aroused in the plexus chakra, Manipura, rises and is transmuted into this love, going beyond gain or loss, the habitual concerns of the ego.

The experience of unconditional love translates into the internal realization of unity with everything, and in that in unity there is nothing different from the sadhaka, everything is his Self; "*Love your neighbor as yourself*" (Matthew 22.39) says Jesus.

The practice of unconditional love can lead sadhaka to the realization of himself in everything:

Without service and love you cannot even dream of attaining advaitic realization even in crones of lives. Service is the expression of love. You serve only when you love man. Knowledge is diffused love and love is concentrated knowledge.

- The Voice of Babaji[1]

The development of consciousness must be balanced with the development of love. Love manifests in compassionate service to others. Consciousness without love can produce an attitude of witness without empathy towards the suffering of others, and much love without consciousness can degenerate into fanaticism, lack of equanimity and lack of discernment.

As consciousness and love expands, we no longer need for the approval of others, nor are we concerned about their opinion of us. The ego usually does the opposite: it seeks to receive the attention, recognition or approval of others, and its expressions of love are limited by the attachments and expectations of something in return.

The higher heart

There is a higher part of the heart, the higher heart, which is linked to unconditional, transpersonal love, beyond the limits of the ego. The opening of the higher heart means an important change in the development of sadhaka. There is no happiness equal to this expansion of love in service to all beings; no meditation can produce this kind of joy.

The opening of the higher heart is a decisive advance in the advancement of sadhak. He or she advances from the perspective of the ego and the desires associated with the lower chakras, engaged in self-interest and in the calculation of gain and loss, to the consciousness of love, occupied in giving, and in which the whole world acquires a new and joyful vision.

To open the heart chakra the sadhaka must eliminate all its blockages and impediments for the free expansion of unconditional love. And almost always this involves resolving past conflicts of the personal history. Many of the blockages of the heart have to do with the feelings of not being loved, disapproval, abandonment - and fear that this can be repeated. No matter what type of therapy we undertake to heal the wounds of the heart, **the acceptance of the past and forgiveness is the ultimate solution to all these conflicts**. Forgiveness is a fundamental tool for healing. Forgiveness does not change the past, but it changes the future: it frees us from the burden of things that have already happened.

Many of the unresolved emotions and hurt feelings we carry are attributed to past experiences from our early childhood days. Those are times when both the aggressor and the victim are ignorant about their words and their actions. Therefore, we must develop the discernment to see their behavior as coming from ignorance. Your precious life and the wholesome development of your inner self is of most importance. The past should never hinder that growth. Forgiveness is not just something that you do for the person who wronged you. It is something you do for your own self. Professionals can only help resolve negative experiences to some degree. Your inner capacity to forgive is the real panacea that can cure past wounds. Let us try to reach a state in which we are able to see all beings on earth as part of our own self and forgive those who have wronged us. This is the path to eternal bliss.

- Amma[2]

Often forgiveness must begin with oneself. Because what we don't accept from others is what we don't accept in us. Accepting and loving ourselves unconditionally, no matter our past and our memories, creates a basis for acceptance and unconditional love for others. If we establish a relationship of acceptance and unconditional love for ourselves then we can establish it with other people.

When any painful or shameful memory of the past comes to you, take this chance to reaffirm your commitment to support and unconditional love for yourself, no matter what happened or what will happen. From there you will allow your love to flow everywhere.

Fears

Fears, that largely shape the personality of the ego, can prevent the opening of the upper heart. All fears are mental constructions. They do not exist in the world, they exist only in the mind of those who experience them.

The opposite of love is fear. The fear anchored in the subconscious is born from the fear that some painful experience of the past could be repeated. It is important to identify and release these fears in the present moment.

Fear is also sustained by the belief in the separation of the Divine, in which there is something apart from Him. The mystic sees the Divine behind everything.

Fear also arises from the lack of surrender of some aspect of our life to the Divine:

For mystics the best cure as soon as one begins to feel afraid of something is to think of the Divine and then snuggle in his arms or at his feet and leave him entirely responsible for everything that happens, within, outside, everywhere—and immediately the fear disappears. That is the cure for the mystic.

- The Mother[3]

The Divine in the heart

The heart chakra is also a center to connect with the Divine. In Bhakti Yoga the sadhaka meditates on the Satguru or divine aspect chosen as residing in his heart, which melts in this form.

The mind is also silenced to hear the intuitive voice of the Satguru, the Divine or the Self itself as a vibration in the heart.

Let the heart, the Inner Man in the heart, guide you, rather than emotion and intellect.

- The Voice of Babaji[4]

Sri Aurobindo places in the heart chakra what he calls "the psychic being," the voice of Self inside us which once unveiled can guide our sadhana and our life:

It (the psychic being) is the seat of the Divine Consciousness, the Divine Self in the individual being. It is a centre of light and truth and knowledge and beauty and harmony which the Divine Self in each of you creates by his presence, little by little; it is influenced, formed and moved by the Divine Consciousness of which it is a part and parcel. It is in each of you the deep inner being which you have to find in order that you may come in contact with the Divine in you. It is the intermediary between the Divine Consciousness and your external consciousness; it is the builder of the inner life, it is that which manifests in the outer nature the order and rule of the Divine Will. If you become aware in your outer consciousness of the psychic being within you and unite with it, you can find the pure Eternal Consciousness and live in it; instead of being moved by the Ignorance as the human being constantly is, you grow aware of the presence of an eternal light and knowledge within you, and to it you surrender and are integrally consecrated to it and moved by it in all things.

(...) Most people are unconscious of this psychic part within them; the effort of Yoga is to make you conscious of it, so that the process of your transformation, instead of a slow labour extending through centuries, can be pressed into one life or even a few years.[5]

The yogic knot of the heart

Yogic texts speak of a *granthi* or knot in the heart. This knot is associated with the breath and the heartbeat. When this knot is dissolved by an advanced yogic practice, the breath and the heartbeat stop in the advanced state of samadhi. The kriya #139, *Om Babaji Sarvikalpa Samadhi Kriya* and other techniques (see "So Ham meditation" in the appendices) help to release that knot, freeing the sadhaka from the attachment to the breath. When the heart knot is loosened through yogic practice, great joy is experienced. The sadhaka must then try to bring this joy to everyday life; in doing so, the bliss of Yoga replaces the dual and limited pleasures of the emotional body.

1- *The Voice of Babaji*, p. 171.
2- Amritanandamyi Devi, Sri Mata. (april 2019) Questions and answers in Sunshine Coast Retreat in Australia. Published in:
https://www.facebook.com/amma.org.nz/posts/amma-speaks-about-forgiveness-and-childlike-innocence-during-the-qa-time-at-the-/2119115631459333/
3- Mother, the. (2003). *Questions and Answers 1953*. Pondicherry: Sri Aurobindo Ashram Publications Department. p. 318.
4- *The Voice of Babaji*, p. 27.
5- Mother, the. (2003). *Questions and Answers 1929-1931*. Pondicherry: Sri Aurobindo Ashram Publications Department. p. 62-63.

The center of the throat and the creative expression

The center of the throat, Vishuddi, is associated with speech and creative self-expression. It can also be a center where the ego constantly manifests and reinforces itself through unnecessary talk or with words of criticism, complaint or disdain.

In Yoga, external and internal silence is very important because it allows us to connect with the source of everything. Silence leaves a space of free of mental movements, which can be subsequently filled by the energy and inspiration of the Self. The practice of silence, *Kriya Mouna Yoga*, serves to calm the mind, restrain the ego and recharge us with energy to all levels, and it is highly recommended in yogic sadhana.

A space of silence is also necessary to integrate life experiences, including the "spiritual experiences" of intense yogic practice, which need to be incorporated into all aspects of our being.

The creative energies within us seek self-expression through the center of the throat. The practice of Yoga does not create uniformity among the sadhak, but rather enhances the individual diversity and the specific potential of each one. Thus, we all have certain talents that can be enhanced by our practice and that we can then put at the service of other beings. Very often yogic silence, Mouna, becomes the source of such creative inspiration.

The Mother, from the ashram of Sri Aurobindo, always encouraged her disciples to do something new and different, to develop their creativity. The higher inspiration we receive through meditations and mantras can help us to develop this creativity.

Devotional chanting is also a magnificent practice that allows the devotional expression and purification of the heart of the devotee and his environment through the vibrations of the mantras or divine names that are sung.

Thus, the center of the neck can be purified and activated by both yogic silence and devotional singing.

The center of the eyebrows and the vision of the light

The door of heaven is in the forehead, in the so-called third eye, between the eyebrows. There is located the Ajna chakra, and when it is activated the yogi sees the Divine everywhere, sees His light in all things:

When your eye is one, your body is filled with light.

- Luke 11.34

The light of the evening, the moon, the sun
The light of the path, the excellent effulgence, the Lord,
Entered me to illumine with wisdom and
Stayed with me enlightening my body.

- Tirumandiram 1529

Brahman, the light of the sky will become
The light of the eye, kudambay!
The light of the eye.

- Siddha Kudambai[1]

When the Yogi constantly thinks that he has a third eye in the middle of his forehead, he perceives a bright and luminous fire. By contemplation in this light, all sins are destroyed, and even the worst person gets the highest end.

If the experienced Yogi thinks of this light day and night, he sees the Siddhas.

- Shiva Samhita V.45-46[2]

In this state of realization of the eyebrows chakra there is still a subtle separation between the yogi and the omnipresent Divine. It is in the crown chakra, Sahasrara, where all separation is dissolved. However, the temporary experience of the samadhi of the crown chakra can create an abyss between that experience and the rest of the daily experiences of the sadhak – this experience can be difficult to be integrated in the daily personality. It is the eyebrows chakra that links heaven and earth, this chakra which reconciles the experience of the Divine of "higher" planes with form. The yogic work for its opening should therefore precede the work of the opening of the crown chakra.

The Ajna chakra is related with the vision of light. Light is the ultimate form of the Divine before its essential aspect of pure Consciousness without any form.

The light is the mystery of the Siddhas, and is widely cited in their works, especially in the Tirumandiram, where Shiva is identified with the shining light experienced by the devotee, first within him and then everywhere.

If one concentrates on the form of light, there is illumination;
If one melts in the light, He will become one with you.

- Tirumandiram 2681

The immense effulgence fills the being as consciousness of direct experience
It goes and comes in the world without tumult
It becomes all pervading effulgence that is beyond speculation.
Who cognizes it? This is the Overlord.

- Tirumandiram 1998

The immense effulgence fills the being as consciousness of direct experience
It goes and comes in the world without tumult

It becomes all pervading effulgence that is beyond
speculation.
Who cognizes it? This is the Overlord.

- Tirumandiram 1998

This light is the vehicle of the manifestation of the Divine, the vehicle of Absolute Consciousness, Shiva. It is sometimes called Nandi, the ox that in the Hindu symbology is the mount of the yogi god:

That light is Nandi.
It becomes the vehicle.
It becomes one limb
of the Sam Veda.

- Siddha Boganathar[3]

The yogi must practice with much patience, perseverance and devotion to dissolve the veil of the third eye, and so the divine light, the light of the Self begins to manifest.

That light is glimpsed when we concentrate all the energy in the head, especially when we transmute the sexual energy into spiritual energy. This transmutation develops the light that corresponds to pure consciousness, the consciousness of the Self. The divinity in the form of Muruga represents this higher consciousness, and his spear represents awakened kundalini and is the celebrated instrument by which He overcame the darkness of ignorance. The Siddha Boganathar, who widely emphasizes this transmutation in his poems, founded two important pilgrimage temples for Muruga in Palani and Katirgama. Muruga has a rooster on his banner, the herald of the light of dawn

The divine light will become more and more visible the more celibacy is practiced and the vital energy is transmuted through the practice of the bandhas, *Brahmacharya Ojas Maitreka Prananyama*, *Kriya Kundalini Pranayama* and the 18 asanas.

The oozing nectar cannot be attained by the lowly;
It will be attained in a second to one who has become a Siva-yogin;
The semen that is arrested will climb up;
The transcendent will clearly appear in the midst of the brows;
The body which is (like) an insect will become shining like the sun;
It is as surprising as walking on the razor's edge!

- Siddha Sundaranandar[4]

The light is also accessed through the practice of continuous awareness, which dissolves the contents of the ego and our identification with them, leaving it free in its own light. That is why the purification of the mind and emotions with the detachment meditations, including those of the nine divine openings as well as the kriyas of samadhi, bring us to effulgent Self awareness, *svarupa*. Of the latter, kriya # 140, *Soruba (Purna) Jyoti Samadhi Dhyana Kriya*, is a direct work with the light - but we must keep in mind that this is facilitated by the practice of the kriyas mentioned - in Babaji's Kriya Yoga the techniques we practice reinforce each other.

The inner light is also made more accessible by our devotional aspiration, as a manifestation of the Divine. **The yogi does not force the appearance of the light; he contemplates it with receptivity and surrender to the divine aspect present in it**.

By grasping, the Light Divine, the Lord,
The Light Divine after being ingrained in me,
Inside the Light Divine I got engrossed and engrossed

And the light Divine declared Its nature.

- Tirumandiram 2842

The light of the divine guru

The Ajna chakra is associated with the light of the divine guru. The sadhaka can focus on him to ask for guidance and advice in his life. In reality there is only one guru, the Divine, who is followed by all the masters and realized beings. The influence of the principle of the guru is made accessible in the third eye, as well as in the center of the heart and in the center of the crown.

When the yogi concentrates on the inner light of the center of the forehead he can, through his devotional aspiration, ask for the guidance of the guru. Through the light the subtle influence of this superior guide can be manifested.

In this sense, Tirumandiram mentions the vision of Shiva's dance in the golden hall of the Chidambaram temple. Chidambaram is the inner light in which the Divine can manifest:

The divine way is the dance-form of
The guru within the cirrambalam

- Tirumandiram 2763

Look steadfastly, front in the forehead;
In the space in between is the luminous mantra;
It is the residence of the Lord, cirrambalam,
Where I am united finally as my grasp and support

- Tirumandiram 2770

Standing as the glowing light is God; by the dazzling light,
The encasing ego is detached from the bonds,

Dancing at the forehead dispels the blemished darkness
He merges as the glowing light at the unmani (mystic center
above the top of the head)

- Tirumandiram 2691

Who can comprehend the spacious wisdom of the divine light
of Sivam
The blissful dancer Sivam; the beautiful dancer Sivam
Of the beautiful word; the dancer at the golden hall;
The dancer at the golden Tillai (Chidambaram); the dancer
of wonder?

- Tirumandiram 2723

The Siddha Ramalinga Swami also speaks of a similar experience, also referring to Chidambaram, the temple hall, the hall of divine knowledge where Shiva dances, and where Ramalinga receives all divine knowledge:

Behold such a unique God
Who shines resplendently
in the sacred Hall of Gnosis in Thillai (Chidambaram).[5]

Oh my Father of great mercy
Who graciously deigned
that I may gain in my early days itself
the gnosis of experiencing You
which comes from contemplation
centred between the eyebrows[6]

It is Civa-chithambaram.
that bestows on them
the clarity which pervades.
the pure heavenly ether of gnosis

which never causes confusion;
it is Civa-chithambaram
which destroys the darkness of ignorance![7]

The transmuting light

The divine light mediates between the Absolute Consciousness, beyond form, and the creation. Siddha Swami Ramalinga speaks of the Divine as the Divine Light of Grace (Arul Perun Jyoti), whose descent made possible the transformation of his physical body into an immortal body of light.

Oh Flame
Who blended with all my body, all my life,
all my mind, all my sentiency,
Who dispelled the darkness (enveloping them) and,
without any rising or setting at any time,
transformed all of them into a blaze of light,
Who, as an embodiment of the rays
Of Civan and Sakti
capable of bestowing anything and everything,
shine in solitary glory
in the middle of the Hall of Gnosis
which is a state of bliss
of unique experience! [8]

Oh resplendent Flame of Thillai (Chidambaram),
Oh Light filling the life
which has entered my fleshly body[9]

Tirumular also speaks of this transformation of the body into light:

If concentrating on the light and chanting clearly

With a melting mind, He will make the body
A golden one by the alchemic pill of Sivayanama

– Tirumandiram 2709

Through the contemplation of the light and the transmutation of the vital energy into spiritual energy a body of light is solidified, capable of receiving and accommodating higher spiritual vibrations that lead to what Sri Aurobindo called "supramental manifestation." This is the ultimate realization of the Siddhas, the Soruba Samadhi or the transformation of the physical body into an immortal divine body, the fruit of sadhana, the absolute surrender of sadhaka and the grace of Divinity.

1- Ganapathy, T. N. (Ed.). (2004). *The Yoga of the 18 Siddhas: An anthology*. St. Etienne de Bolton, Quebec: Babaji's Kriya Yoga and Publications. p.327.

2- Chandra Vasu, S. (tras.). (1914). *Siva Samhita*. Allahabad: The Panini Office, Bhuvanesware Asrama, Bahadurganj.

3- Little, L. Shaking the Tree: *Kundalini Yoga, Spiritual Alchemy, & the Mysteries of the Breath in Bhogar's 7000*. Verse 50. Available in:
   https://www.alchemywebsite.com/bhogar.html

4- *The Yoga of the 18 Siddhas: An anthology*, p. 255.

5- *Pathway to God Trod by Saint Ramalingar*, p.308.

6- Id., p.397.

7- Id., p.287-289.

8- Id., p.390-391.

9- Id., p.268.

The center of the crown and Ultimate Oneness

The complete opening of Sahasrara, the crown chakra, is the culmination of spiritual practice, and is equivalent to what is known as *nirvikalpa samadhi*, absorption without differences in the Self.

As we saw before, when the Ajna chakra or third eye opens the yogi sees the Divine everywhere, he sees His light in all things. However, there is still separation between the yogi and the omnipresent Divine. It is in the crown chakra, Sahasrara, where all separation is dissolved and the experience of the One without a second is achieved in the union of nirvikalpa samadhi or union / absorption without differences. That is why the saints are represented in different traditions with the halo around the head, representing the opening of that center.

It can be said that the activation and experience of the Ajna chakra corresponds to the experience of the Divine in form, and the experience of the Sahasrara chakra corresponds with the experience of God, the Self or the All, without any other point of view other than him: the experience of the One.

The one reveals Himself as many and the many are in essence one. Realize the Bliss of Oneness and the joy of many. Just as one who cannot speak, cannot describe the taste of sugar candy, so also no one can describe the beauty, glory and Bliss of Brahman. You will have to realize them yourself through nirvikalpa samadhi.

- The Voice of Babaji[1]

Spiritual architecture

The temple of Tanjore, South India, has a 66-meter tower crowned with an 80-ton stone. It is a building that amazes current engineers. The Siddha Karuvurar was responsible for its construction. King Raja Chola was so pleased with his work that he had a shrine erected in honor of Siddha in the temple, where his image can be seen today.

The tower is a good metaphor for the Yoga of the Siddhas. Its practitioners concentrate the vital energy at the top of the head, in order to open the crown chakra. This is the chakra of union with the Absolute. **This experience of union or "samadhi" is only sustainable if the yogi has created an internal structure that supports it**, which includes the purification of the energy channels and the subconscious and the activation of the other centers of consciousness or chakras. The kriyas or techniques are used for this, through postures, breaths, meditations and mantras.

You cannot start a house on the roof - the roof is the final culmination of the effort in building a home.

Life, in all its many aspects, is a divine manifestation. **Fulfilling these different aspects is the task of sadhaka, manifested in the purification of the *chitta* and the nadis and in the activation of the chakras**. The sadhaka must fulfill the different experiences of life that he needs to face, concretized in each of the seven chakras and their corresponding learning, before arriving at the experience without return of the One.

Just escaping from than life, fleeing to the crown chakra is not the way of the Siddhas. Sadhana must be performed in all the chakras, including the seventh, in a balanced way, as explained in the chapter "The advanced practice of activating the chakras." Thus, an energetic, mental and emotional base must be created that could sustain the experience of the opening of the crown chakra. And the foundation of that base is the subconscious of the sadhaka, which must be purified through his yogic practice.

Full devotional and vital surrender is also necessary before being able to advance to samadhi or absorption in the crown chakra. This delivery implies, among other things, that the sadhaka learns to see the Divine in everything that surrounds him and in everything that happens to him.

Full devotional and vital surrender are also necessary before being able to advance into samadhi or absorption in the crown chakra. This surrender implies, among other things, that the sadhaka learns to see the Divine in everything that surrounds him and in everything that happens to him.

Samadhi, absorption in the Self

The crown chakra is related with the state of samadhi. Samadhi is the dissolution, first temporary, and then definitive, of the "I" in pure consciousness. The Yoga Sutras of Patanjali make a classification of different types of samadhi. In Babaji's Kriya Yoga we define samadhi as "the breathless state of union with God or the Absolute."

Samadhi is usually distinguished into two types, *savikalpa* (with differences) and *nirvikalpa* (without differences). In the first, the sadhaka experiences a temporary state of absorption in the Self but his ego is still there, maintaining its features. In the second there is the absolute absorption of sadhaka in the Self, the house of his ego is burned and its dissolution occurs. There remains only the Self, without differences.

Nirvikalpa samadhi is also divided into two types, *kevala* and *sahaja*.

There are two nirvikalpa samadhis, the yogic samadhi called the kevala nirvikalpa *and the* samadhi *of the sage (jnani), which is called the* sahaja nirvikalpa. *In the former, the yogi's mind is temporarily merged in the* chaitanya *(consciousness) if the Self and can be brought back to the world as a bucket with a rope tied to it an let down into a well can be drawn out of the well by the rope. In the latter, the sage's mind is once for all dissolved and lost in the real Self, like a river that has become one with the ocean, and hence cannot revive and turn back to the world. But this* sahaja *(natural) state does not hinder the sage from unchaining automatically in the world. Nor does this functioning hinder the sage from remaining in his state of awareness of the real Self. It would seem that though the sage's mind is dissolved in the real Self, there is an attenuated remnant of the mind, which can function, being activated by God Himself by His mere presence.*

- The Voice of Babaji[2]

Sahaja samadhi corresponds to what people call "enlightenment," it is the irrevocable state of realization of Self. Until you getting there the yogi can experience samadhis, or even develop yogic powers, but he has not reached the final goal, and he can make mistakes that impede or stop completely his progress.

Sahaja samadhi is the true state of deliverance from bondage and from ignorance. This is the supreme state beyond which there is nothing higher to be realized, and hence, it alone, is the goal of religious endeavor.

- The Voice of Babaji[3]

Traditional yogis often abandon matter to go to samadhi. The Siddhantam, the Yoga of the Siddhas, brings samadhi even to matter, to the cells of the physical body.

The point of absortion in the Divine

In Yoga, the Sahasrara chakra is considered as the exit door of this physical plane; the yogi climbs the ladder of spiritual realization to achieve liberation from the endless cycle of reincarnations.

The highest elevation to attain is the Jnan Chakra, when the Yogi becomes "face to face" with the all pervasive spirit the Brahma – the Ultimate Creative Force, and becomes "knower of Brahma", a Brahmavit. At this stage he becomes endowed with all Vibhutis and powers of a Master Yogi.[4]

It is difficult to find references about the experience of nirvikalpa samadhi in the crown chakra, probably because the fusion with Pure Consciousness is alien to every experience of the phenomenal world and to every experience of the mind. The Siddhas, like the mystics of various traditional spirituals, express such experience of absorption in the Self with the poetic language of their verses.

In this rest-hall there is only day; no darkness.
Nor is there any need to raise a fire.
If this is realized, it becomes easy to prolong.
As there is no night, there is no dawn either.

- Siddha Tirumular[5]

There is neither "I" nor you, nor he, in that Stupendous Silence. There is neither East nor West, neither day nor night in that Light of Lights. Brahman walks without feet, hears without ears, sings without tongue, tastes without mouth, grasps without hands. There is neither air nor fire, neither earth nor sky, neither sun nor moon. The pairs of opposites do not exist there. There is neither pleasure nor pain, neither love nor hatred, neither doubt nor delusion in the Kingdom of God. There the trees bear fruits of immortality. There the rivers flow with the elixir of Bliss.

- The voice of Babaji[6]

Sri Aurobindo describes nirvikalpa samadhi with these words: *"In more scientific parlance it is a trance in which there is no formation or movement of the consciousness and one gets lost in a state from which one can bring back no report except that one was in bliss."* [7]

We find in his work "Synthesis of Yoga" the following description:

Beyond a certain point the trance becomes complete and it is then almost or quite impossible to awaken or call back the soul that has receded into them (...) There are said to be supreme states of trance in which the soul persisting for too long a time cannot return; for it loses its hold on the cord which binds it to the consciousness of life, and the body is left, maintained indeed in its set position, not dead by dissolution, but incapable of recovering the ensouled life which had inhabited it.[8]

The point of the descent of the Divine

In the Yoga of the Siddhas the crown chakra can be the point of absorption in the Self and also the point of descent of the Divine into the lower vehicles of the sadhaka, the intellectual, mental, vital and physical bodies. The Sahasrara center is the place where lotus feet of the Divine or the Satguru are located, and from them their transforming Grace descends to this plane.

My Lord has bestowed (me) the head at the time of holding the feet;
Granted the sword of knowledge and its strength:
And the reign over the house without end;

Placed on the head the crown of grace by descending on the earth.

- Tirumandiram 1591

The wisdom of the holy feet will change (ne) into the essence of Sivam.
The wisdom of the holy feet will reach me to Siva's place;
The wisdom of the holy feet will release me from the prison of impediments
The wisdom of the holy feet is the mighty siddhi and mukti *too.*

- Tirumandiram 1598

The expression "seeking refuge at the feet of the Divine / Guru" thus has an esoteric meaning in the texts of the Siddhas. From them, from Sahasrara, the transforming divine Grace descends to this plane, which ultimately leads to the final perfection (*siddhi*) of Soruba Samadhi, the ultimate achievement of the Siddhas.

The redoubtable dhyana sloka (meditation verse) *for self-surrender is "Salutations to you, O great Yogin (Babaji). Pray, direct me who has fallen at your Feet, so that I may find unfailing delight in your Lotus Feet".*

- The Voice of Babaji[9]

The sage of yore kept the feet of the guru
On their crown and attained grace;
The aim of those who follow the path is
To attain the flood of the sweet fruit of the feet.

- Tirumandiram 1603

In truth the joy is unlimited to those who have reached the feet;

The celestials who are the crowned kings turned into
Vassals of the Lord and became free from blemishes.

- Tirumandiram 1601

In Babaji's Kriya Yoga we also honor the guru in the crown chakra in the Salutation Pose, in the Science of Sun Worship pose and in the fourth phase of *Kriya Kundalini Pranayama*.

For his part, Sri Aurobindo comments from his teaching of Integral Yoga:

The highest organised centre of our embodied being and of its action in the body is the supreme mental centre figured by the yogic symbol of the thousand-petalled lotus, sahasradala, and it is at its top and summit that there is the direct communication with the supramental levels. It is then possible to adopt a different and a more direct method, not to refer all our thought and action to the Lord secret in the heart-lotus but to the veiled truth of the Divinity above the mind and to receive all by a sort of descent from above, a descent of which we become not only spiritually but physically conscious. [10]

Sri Aurobindo also points out that Kundalini or the Divine Force is also above our head, as a fully awaked energy, and can be invoked by the sadhak, which can be transformed when this Divine Force descends into him.

But it (Kundalini Shakti) is also above us, above our head as the Divine Force – not there coiled up, involved, asleep, but awake, scient, potent, extended and wide; it is there waiting for manifestation and to this Force we have to open ourselves – to the power of the Mother. (...) It can pour downwards to the body, working, establishing its reign, extending into wideness from above, link the lowest in us with the highest above us, release the individual into a cosmic universality or into absoluteness and transcendence. [11]

Sri Aurobindo mentions that in the head there is a golden lid, which once it breaks, allows the direct descent of all divine influence.

Above the Mind there is not only the Infinite in itself but an infinite sea of peace, joy, light, power, etc. The golden lid - Hiranmaya patra - intervenes between that which is above Mind and what is below. Once one can break that lid those elements can come down at any time one wills, and for that, quietude is necessary. [12]

The object of the ascension is for the lower nature to join the higher consciousness so that (1) the limit or lid between the higher and the lower may be broken and disappear, (2) the consciousness may have free access to higher and higher planes, (3) a free way may be made for the descent of the higher Consciousness into the lower planes. [13]

We find that the Siddhas mention this realization in their poems with different words:

To preserve the body, open the lid,
The lid is opened by Hatha Yoga;
The human body considered as an appearance is the gateway;
By reversing the many bonded body make it the truth and achieve victory.

- Siddha Boganathar[14]

The complete practice of Hatha Yoga, belonging to Tantra tradition - the latest development of Yoga - includes asanas, bandhas and pranayamas, in order to clean the nadis, activate the chakras and finally direct and concentrate the vital energy on the top of the head. The purpose is to open the upper chakras with it.

In the texts of the Siddhas and in the teaching of Sri Aurobindo this opening allows the descent of the transforming Grace from the feet of the Divine in the Sahasrara chakra.

O! Ye who have realized the junction of the four
Having reached the crown in search of the cause!
Having seen the door above open
The term death is not even in your dreams.

- Siddha Tirumular[15]

Converging in silence, if the mind is stilled,
It acquires a taintless form; the delusion has disappeared;
Being engrossed in the Absolute in concentration,
It has become possible to descend manifesting grace.

- Siddha Sundaranandar[16]

If you can search for the feet of the Lord day and night, oh!
Cow!
The realized state will come to you and you will see the
Perfect One, oh! Cow!

- Siddha Idai Kadar[17]

Idai Kadar, the Siddha who was a shepherd, uses the term "cow" (*pasu* in Tamil) referring to the individual soul. In the lotus feet of the Divine the soul will see Perfection (*siddhi*). Reaching there the state of Shiva is what turns the yogi into a Siddha (perfected being).

The ultimate attainment

The activation of the crown chakra is then decisive for the realization of the Self of the sadhak, whether he dissolves forever his individuality in the *nirvikalpa samadhi*, in search of the final liberation, or if it becomes the door of descent of the Divine, to his transformation into the Soruba Samadhi, the final achievement of the Siddhas.

The sadhaka will decide at a given moment, from his freedom, the final path he wishes to choose in his realization.

The Mother cannot decide for you, she can only offer to you the Truth she has come here to bring to the world and, if you accept it, guide you towards it.

- The Mother[18]

1- *The Voice of Babaji*, p. 229.

2- Id., p. 159-160.

3- Id., p. 157.

4- Bejoy Dasgupta, Sri Sailendra. (2006). *Kriya Yoga.* iUniverse. Chapter V.

5- *The Yoga of the 18 Siddhas: An Anthology*, p. 87.

6- *The Voice of Babaji*, p. 228.

7- Aurobindo, Sri. (2005). *Letters on Yoga.* Pondicherry: Sri Aurobindo Ashram Publications Department. p. 752.

8- Aurobindo, Sri. (1999). *The Synthesis of Yoga.* Pondicherry: Sri Aurobindo Ashram Publications Department. p. 521.

9- *The Voice of Babaji*, p. 463.

10- *The Synthesis of Yoga*, p. 805.

11- *The Integral Yoga*, p. 221.

12- Purani, A.B. (1995). *Evening talks with Sri Aurobindo.* Pondicherry: Sri Aurobindo Society. p. 578.

13- Aurobindo, Sri. (2014). *Letters on Yoga III.* Pondicherry: Sri Aurobindo Ashram Publications Department. p. 430.

14- *The Yoga of the 18 Siddhas: An anthology*, p. 111.

15- Id., p. 98.

16- Id., p. 304.

17- Id., p. 378.

1- 18- Aurobindo, Sri. (2012). *The Mother with Letters on the Mother.* Pondicherry: Sri Aurobindo Ashram Publications Department. p. 333.

The Grace of the 18 Siddhas

The integration of the Divine in the form

The yoga of the Siddhas is the culmination of the tantric yogic tradition, the perfect union of Shiva and Shakti, consciousness and energy, matter and spirit. You can have the realization of the Divine completely detached from the form, but the achievement of Babaji and the Siddhas implies the perfect integration of the Divine into it.

In his great work "Savitri" Sri Aurobindo describes the realization of those who embody the supramental consciousness or Consciousness-Truth on earth. A description that could apply to the 18 Siddhas:

> *Some shall be made the glory's receptacles*
> *And vehicles of the Eternal's luminous power.*
> *These are the high forerunners, the heads of Time,*
> *The great deliverers of earth-bound mind,*
> *The high transfigurers of human clay,*
> *The first-born of a new supernal race.*
> *The incarnate dual Power shall open God's door,*
> *Eternal supermind touch earthly Time.*
> *The superman shall wake in mortal man*
> *And manifest the hidden demigod*
> *Or grow into the God-Light and God-Force*
> *Revealing the secret deity in the cave.*[1]

The Siddhas, since their ineffable realization and transformation, continue to live for the transformation of humanity, guiding a few and inspiring many. They are comparable to the bodhisattvas of the Buddhist tradition:

Each of the 18 Siddhas has made significant contributions to the world of science, medicine, literature, yoga and philosophy. They work anonymously behind the scenes, inspiring and assisting seekers in all fields of endeavour. In so doing, they assist humanity's evolution towards a higher universal consciousness.

- Marshall Govindan[2]

In fact, service to humanity is a key concept in the philosophy of the Sidddhas:

The arru-p-padai concept, that we find in Tamil literature, that is, "the concept of directing or showing the path to one and all," irrespective o caste, creed, sex, religion or nationality, has acquired a socio-philosophical meaning at the hands of the Siddhas. It is a concept emphasizing the vow of helping humanity by one's own enlightenment. Their songs are indicators of the path of self-realization for the seeker after truth. The Siddhas wanted everyone to enjoy what they themselves have enjoyed. They have a loving desire to secure the welfare, happiness and solidarity to all beings. In Siddha mysticism humanity and not God is the point of reference. The arru-p-padai concept (the method of showing the way) is an expression of the mysticism of the Siddhas in that it is their commitment to humanity to indicate the pathway. This concept of the Siddhas to pass on the torch of spirituality to other men is the highest altruistic action. They sincerely felt that genuine freedom is not in isolation.[3]

Each of the 18 Siddhas had a different realization in the Divine, primarily embodying different spiritual qualities. As a review, we can attribute to each of them - in a non-exhaustive way, of course - these various qualities:

Tirumular - Yogic wisdom
Rama Devar - Mantras, transformation of the vital

Agastyar - Force, protection
Konkanavar - Receptivity
Kamala Muni - Silence
Sattamuni - Aspiration and descent of Grace
Karuvurar - Bases for spirituality
Sundaranandar - Light and beauty
Valmiki - Surrender
Nandi Devar - Knowledge of Shiva
Paambati - Kundalini
Boganathar - Wisdom and discernment
Macchamuni - Tantra
Patanjali - The Seer, witness consciousness
Dhanvantri - Spiritual healing
Goraknath - Detachment, yogic *tapas*
Kudambai - Devotion
Idai Kadar - Light of inner Self

These 18 Siddhas are recognized in the Siddhantha tradition of southern India, but there are many more, especially recognized in the state of Tamil Nadu, the region where this tradition arose. Other famous Siddhas are Avvai, Roma Rishi, Kalangi, Sivavakiyar, Pattinathar, Pulastiyar, Punaikannar and Pulipanni.

Mantras of Grace

Although they are rarely physically accessible, the Siddhas are accessible through our sincere devotion and in meditation. Their grace is more available than it may seem, but one must be prepared to receive it. Yogic sadhana makes the sadhak more and more receptive to their influence.

The student of Babaji's Kriya Yoga can receive the mantras of each of the 18 Siddhas and also learn to meditate on them. These mantras recapitulate their spiritual realization. When the sadhak repeats them he incorporates the qualities developed by the invoked Siddha. The mantras of the Siddhas not only serve to tune into them, but also to incorporate their spiritual achievement and to spread their vibration everywhere.

Raising the aspiration, receiving Grace

The invocation of divine Grace and its descent permeates the poems of the Siddhas.

In the practice of the asanas of Kriya Yoga we invoke it in the first asana, the Salutation to the guru, and in the second asana, when we sing the Song of the Science of Sun Worship.

An old debate in spirituality is whether we should depend on Grace or our own effort for our spiritual advancement. The answer may be that we must depend on both.

A good metaphor for understanding Grace and our efforts to receive it would be to think of a water tap. If we want to receive water from it we must put ourselves underneath it. If we want to receive the grace of a guru or the Divine we need to humbly replace the ego's perspective and place ourselves under them with aspiration and receptivity.

Our aspiration of the heart is what allows us to open the tap of Grace and that it flows over us. The Mother affirms: "*All sincere prayers are granted, every call is answered.*" [4]

The emptier the container is under the tap, the more it can be filled with water. The more we empty ourselves of our little "I", the more space we leave for Grace to enter.

If there is dirt inside the container, the water, like the grace that descends, will remove this dirt from the sadhaka. At first the entire container will be filled with dirty water. But if you allow water to continue to pour into the container, it becomes clean.

If there are holes in the vessel, the waters of Grace will be lost. These "holes" are our usual tendencies that disperse and waste the energy received through: anger, moodiness, desires and other emotions

The six-pointed star appears in the *yantras* of the Siddhas, especially in the yantras of Lord Muruga. His yantra can be accompanied by six syllables that constitute another of Muruga's names: *Sha ra va na bha va* - which literally means "I take refuge with devotion." This star is formed by the intersection of two triangles; the triangle that points up represents our aspiration and our efforts for attaining Grace, and the triangle that points down represents its descent into us.

Uniting Heaven and Earth

In the path of the Siddhas, samadhi, the union with the Self, is brought even to our physical cells. Ultimately, according to Siddhantha, the teachings of the Siddhas, samadhi needs not become merely the exit door of *samsara*, the endless cycle of reincarnations, but the door of divine descent into what we call "matter." Matter is energy, the manifestation of the divine Shakti. In the realization of the Siddhas, Spirit and matter lose their original separation, they reconcile and become one.

Our aspiration, our work to transmute and raise our energies and our kundalini is like a stalagmite. The descent of inspiration, guidance, energy and transforming Grace are the stalagmite. Both must eventually unite and create a bridge that links heaven and earth.

The ancient realization of the Siddhas has now become, as explained by Sri Aurobindo and the Mother, the next evolutionary advance of humanity. Our progress and realization on the path of the Siddhas is an advance of all, and not only for humans, but for all sentient beings, at critical moments of transition of our planet. Babaji said that we not only do Kriya Yoga for our good, but for others.

1- Aurobindo, Sri. (2017). *Savitri: A legend and a symbol.* Pondicherry: Sri Aurobindo Ashram Publication Department. p. 705.

2- Govindan, M. (1993). *Babaji and the 18 Siddha Kriya Yoga tradition.* St. Etienne de Bolton, Quebec: Babaji's Kriya Yoga and Publications. p. 30.

3- *The Yoga of the 18 Siddhas.* p.8.
4- Mother, the. (2004). *Words of the Mother III.* Pondicherry: Sri Aurobindo Ashram Publications Department. p. 208.

Texts of the Siddhas: Kudambai

*To those who have climbed to the top of the hill and drunk the
fresh mango juice*
What is the use of coconut juice? Kudambay!
What is the use of coconut juice?

- Siddha Kudambay[1]

Aspiration is the longing of our heart of uniting,
unconditionally, with the Divine. Sri Aurobindo states that God
always responds to the sincere aspiration of the devotee, and
therefore, this is the main requisite to advance in the realization
of the Divine.

Jesus said: *"Love the Lord your God with all your heart and with all your soul and with all your strength and with all your mind,"* Luke 10.27.

In Babaji's Kriya Yoga aspiration manifests and takes form by concentrating all the vital energy ("all your strength"), at the feet of the Divine.

The effort of the yogi, in the path of the Siddhas, is rising and concentrating his vital energy in one point, the crown *chakra* in the top of the head, through *asanas*, *bandahs* (muscular locks), meditations, and above all, *pranayamas* – the technique most emphasized by the Siddhas.

Even the devotion for the Divine has the effect of raising the vital energy upwards, to the crown *chakra* – we can see this even in the images of the Christian saints, with their gaze upwards and a corolla around their heads.

Sahasrara, the crown chakra, is an essential place in the subtle anatomy of the human being, widely mentioned by the Siddhas in their poems. Sometimes it is referred to as *the abode of Shiva*, *the Mount Meru* or *Kailash*, the top of the mountain or the feet of the Divine. This last image of the feet at the *sahasrara chakra* is used very often to refer to the place where the grace of God flows, and in India the devotees touch the feet of their *gurus* to receive their blessings and grace. The crown *chakra* is also the place of meeting and fusion between the devotee and the Divine, the place where *"the jiva becomes Shiva"* – the individual becomes one with the Divine (*"The Father and I are one,"* John 10.30).

The concept of "grace" is plentiful also in the poems of the Siddhas and refers to the answer of the Divine to the longing of the devotee for Him. *Sadhana* or spiritual discipline includes all those yogic practices done in order to get closer to the Divine. This includes our receptivity to the descent of His grace – His answer to our call. Yogic sadhana is a preparation of receptivity for such grace, to become a vessel without leaks, to recognize it and to preserve it, without wasting it in the habits of the ego, who is usually interested in recognition, pleasure or power: *"And no one pours new wine into old wineskins. If he does, the new wine will burst the skins and will be spilled, and the skins will be destroyed"* (Luke 5.37).

Descent

Through devotional aspiration, the buildup of vital energy and concentration and meditation in the feet of the Divine, the crown *chakra*, we could experience the response of the Divine to the soul's call: the descent of His grace.

The concentration of the mind upwards sends a rush of this force through the top of the head and the response comes in a fine rain of soft magnetism. The feeling arising from the downward power sends a wonderful glow through the body and one feels as if he is bathed in a kind of soft electricity.

- The Voice of Babaji. [2]

The more intense is our meditation, the state of mental silence, and our devotional longing, the more intense will be this response. The *sadhaka* could perceive different impressions including light, deep peace, insights, and contentment of the heart. Of all them, the most important and desirable one – as the phenomena such as visions are only passing experiences, however unusual or subtle – is to receive the bliss of the Self. In India God is defined a *Sat-Chit-Ananda*, absolute Being-Consciousness-Bliss. Bliss, the unconditional joy that fulfills the heart, is the Presence of the Divine. This is what we all are looking for, in vain, through the senses.

Therefore, the meaning of the poem of Kudambay:

What is the use of coconut juice?

The coconut is the symbol of our ego, our little "I," the result of our identification with our body, our emotions and our mind. The hard shell of this fruit that unites its many fibers is like our habit of identification with them. The *coconut juice* represents the fleeting pleasures of the ego.

The *mango juice* represents the sweetness of the Self, manifested from the crown *chakra* (*"the top of the hill"*), a sweetness or bliss that fulfills the longing of the devotee for experiencing the Divine, making him forget the limited and fleeting pleasures that the ego pursues in this world. Yogananda defined God as "ever new joy;" a bliss that never bores the devotee, unlike the sense, emotional and mental pleasures, that, being dual, finally produce weariness.

For our daily sadhana:

As sadhaks of Yoga, we should "bring the *samadhi* to our daily life and not our daily life to the *samadhi*." This means that we should extend the peace and the bliss obtained by our meditation and our yogic practice to our daily life, to transform it, and we shouldn't let the problems of our daily life disturb our meditation.

The Siddha Kudambay encourages us to practice the divine Presence in our life, drinking the bliss from the *sahasrara chakra*, the feet of the Divine. Practicing *sadhana*, before and after our working day, helps us on this, together with moments of remembrance of the feet of the Divine in the top of our head. By doing so we bring down the deep joy of the Divinity, and all the beings around us also benefit from this, in one way or another. Thus our life becomes a life worthy of being lived.

1- *The Yoga of the 18 Siddhas.* p. 354.
2- *The Voice of Babaji.* p. 459.

Texts of the Siddhas: essence of the Tirumandiram

Tirumandiram, a book written by the Tirumular Siddha, is probably the most important text in the of the 18 Siddhas tradition of South India. The work consists of 3,000 verses of verses with all the knowledge of Yoga and Tantra of the time, a fundamental work of Yoga.

The section of 30 verses of Tirumandiram ranging from 113 to 142, included, is titled "Ubdecam", which means "Instruction in essence." As explained in the book *"English translation of the Tirumandiram"*[1]:

Ubadecam is a set of instructions the teacher imparts to the disciple. The instructions include those of an esoteric kind and demand the disciple understand their significance in depth, and most importantly, adopt them for guuidance in personal experience. These instructions have a large element of anubhava (experiential) content. This experience is not of a sensory type based on body-sense-mind related to external or even internal matters. The anubhava (experience) is of a spiritual kind the soul encounters the intercession of the Lord's grace. The Lord's grace as experienced by the guru is transmitted to the disciple through instructions, which assume a divine character. Arunai Vadivel Mudaliyar says the verses in the "Ubadecam" section are of a character brought about by the arul (grace) Tirumular has experienced within himself, resulting in the truths he is stating, and therefore these verses are of immense value to the disciple and every practicing spiritual aspirant:

Lord, descending, takes on forms appropriate to the deeds;
His grace, He has positioned for my protection before long;
My heart, He melts abiding with; Great Bliss, He does;
With His grace, make me experience; the verdigris, He has removed.

The blemish He cut asunder, our Nandi[2] with the third eye;
The eye of grace opened within; the rust He removed;
The effulgent light that He showed, impurity nears not;
My Lord it is, the coral He inlaid with the crystal.

God, soul and bondage, the three they speak of;
Like God, soul and bondage, too, are beginningless;
Soul and bondage near not God;
Let God approach, bondage stays not.

Like the indwelling fire that rises from the bamboo,
In the temple of this body, is seated our Lord Nandi;
The three impurities, He sets aside with compassion stronger

than mother's
That floods like the rising sun.

Sunstone and cotton wrapped around it are alike;
Sunstone burns not, the wrapped cotton;
Sunstone burns the cotton in sun's presence
When guru appears, destroyed are the impurities.

The blemishes five He destroyed, His grace bestowed,
Sadasiva is He, of the five sacred states;
Five senses He set at naught, Nandi, the dancer;
As sacred letters five, His grace came to abide in me.

The soul bound by the sense,
Drown in waters deep, not knowing the way;
When the way is taught by the teacher Supreme,
Submerged is the soul's consciousness in Consciousness
great.

Like the swan that separates cow's milk from water,
The Lord's exclusive dance of grace on the unique stage
Does separate the karma of the evil instruments
And burn up the seed that causes birth.

The seed, they destroy, their level of consciousness
is suddha-turiya, free from atachment,
Harmonious are their senses and experience;
While living, dead in body, are the Siva-yogins.

Siva-Yoga distinguishes cit from acit.
Penance of Yoga-deep, Siva's effulgence in one's own self,
Shunning wrong paths; great bliss of love delights;
New Yoga this is! Nandi gave us.

He revealed the truth of His immanence;
His world, the celestials knew not, He showed;
The sacred feet of the holy dance, He placed on me;

He bestowed the great bliss of the gracious space.

Pervasiveness finds its place in omniscience;
Love settles in grace;
Inner light, with divine effulgence intermingled;
Serene are the Siva-Siddhas in their clarity.

Siddhas perceive the Siva-loka here;
They experience within, nada[3] and Nadanta[4].
They are eternal, pure and blemishless;
Liberated they are, from tattvas[5] thirty-six.

The thirty-six steps of the ladder of liberation, they ascend;
The incomparable bliss of the inner light of grace is theirs;
The indescribable Siva, they saw with clarity
And abided in Sivahood.

Abiding in Sivahood, they were here and everywhere;
Comprehend, they could, all Siva's activity;
The three-fold aspect of time, they knew to look into;
Their's the loss; they gain serenity of inaction.

In space-pure, are the serene;
In space-pure, abide the serene;
Beyond the Vedas extends the consciousness of the serene;
The serene experience the supreme, indifferent to the Vedas.

Asleep, they perceive the world of Siva within themselves;
Asleep, they perceive the Siva-Yoga within themselves;
Asleep, they experience the bliss of Siva within themselves;
The greatness of such serene ones; can it be described?

As He sees extent of one's progress,
So will He bestow His grace, primal Siva;
As Uma enjoys, He dances in the assembly
Like the wise sun in the fair sky, flaming like ruby.

Like the lustrous emerald encased within the ruby,
Like emerald mansion set in the ruby,
In the divine dance in the assembly of finest gold;
Worshipping Him thus, what a boon they receive!

Recipients are they, in this world, of the great way;
Recipients are they, in this world, of the reward of
birthlessness;
Recipients are they of the boon of eternal closeness;
Recipients are they of the power of silence in the world.

Like our Lord knows greatness and smallness
And to be rare or to be easy, whoever knows
So, tortoise-like, withdrawing its limb unto itself;
They remain, blemishless, unconcerned about this world or
the next.

Like the ghee that lies latent in pure milk,
When the teacher's word settles in clear mind
And becomes an experience, even as the soul departs,
Unites with intimate effulgence, and remains in eminence.

The senses five will go back to their kind;
Where will the soul rest, but in the supreme intelligence?
In pure space, the small flame will merge with the large one;
Know this to be grace of the teacher.

The sharp sun rays heat up the water;
The name and form of salt, so they create;
Put in water again, salt becomes one with the water;
So it is that the soul gets dissolved into Siva.

Universe, the atom settles in it;
A different universe, it does not go to; is there another place?
Should the embodied soul decide to reach its shore,
It is the holy feet on one who stands with assurance.

Holy feet is Siva, when you inquire;
Holy feet is Siva-loka, when you reflect;
Holy feet is the path to take, if you but say;
Holy feet is the refuge for those who are clear.

Illuminating it is, to perceive guru's sacred person;
Illuminating it is, to chant guru's sacred name;
Illuminating it is, to listen to guru's sacred word;
Illuminating it is, to reflect on the guru's person.

Senses five come under one's own charge;
Senses five will lose their power;
Senses five will change their course,
When one has placed oneself before one's Lord.

Nandi's sacred feet, I am conjoined with;
Nandi's sacred person, I ponder over;
Nandi's sacred name, I chant;
Nandi's golden teaching remains in my mind.

Holy they became, who in their mind
Kept the holy Nandi, the giver of wisdom;
Perceiving His dance, eyes filled with rapture,
As the Vedas sang their praise, supreme space they reached.

1- *The Tirumandiram, Volume 1*. p. 148.
2- *Nandi*: another name for Shiva; also, the guru of Tirumular.
3- *Nada*: divine sound, Om.
4- *Nadanta*: consciousness beyond the Om sound.
5- *Tattvas*: elements of Nature.
6- *Uma*: the wife (shakti or energy) of Siva.
7- *Siva-loka*: world of Siva.

Appendices: considerations about the yogic practice

Meditation in "Om Kriya Babaji Nama Aum"

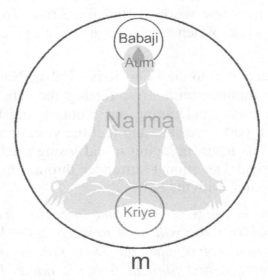

Om Kriya Babaji Nama Aum

"Nama" means "salutation, I bow to". It stands for surrender. In Babaji's Kriya Yoga surrender is practiced by the concentration of all our vital energy in the crown chakra, through devotion and the yogic kriyas. This attainment can facilitate the descent of a Higher Consciousness.

"Kriya" means "action with awareness". Kriya Shakti is the energy of action. "Kriya" also stands for Kundalini, the primordial energy in the base of the spine. The practices of Kriya Yoga produce a gradual, never sudden, awakening of Kundalini; in its ascent towards the crown chakra Kundalini brings forth to the surface our inner tendencies that impedes its rise. So, Kriya Yoga activatess and requires a process of purification from the sadhak.

"Babaji" means "revered Father." It equals the "Heavenly Father" of the words of Jesus, the Supreme Consciousness that upholds the universe. We all have the potential to realize this Consciousness in the crown chakra. This Consciousness gets more and more activated as Kundalini is more and more able to reach this chakra. So, the mantra "Om Kriya Babaji Nama Aum" recapitulates the yogic work in Babaji's Kriya Yoga, and also activates this work. When we repeat it we are practicing Kriya Yoga!

A great practice is to sing Om Kriya Babaji Nama Aum for 15, 20 or 30 minutes with love, feeling the vibration of the mantra in the body, and giving our whole being to the song. Then - the best part - we stop and feel the vibration and energy that the song left in us, enjoying it and losing track of time. A very joyful kriya! Devotional surrender through the name is a direct path to union with the Self.

O man, why do you waste your time in gossip? You will have to repent in old age. You will have to weep at the hour of your death. Have a rich crop of japa *now. Do not argue, do not doubt. Have full reverence and faith in Babaji's name. His name is nectar and that is your prop. Cross this* samsara *with Satguru Deva's name! Ramdas, Tukaram and Narsi Mehta, Jnana Deva, Nama Dey and Damaji practiced* japa *and attained God-realization. Name is an asset for you. Name is real wealth for you, if you repeat the name one thousand times. You will have immense spiritual wealth in the spiritual bank of Babaji!"*

- The Voice of Babaji [1]

1- *The Voice of Babaji*, p. 483.

Yoga Nidra: the importance of being awake

Nidra Yoga is an extremely powerful technique in Babaji's Kriya Yoga, but often not appreciated by students. In the practice of Yoga Nidra we try to remain as the witness in the face of fluctuations in consciousness, and we go through different mental states: from the waking state to the daydreaming, and then to the dreamless state of sleep. In Yoga Nidra the sadhaka can reach the state of *turiya*, beyond these three: *turiya* is the primordial state of consciousness, its foundation, beyond waking, dreaming and sleeping. Reaching the state of *turiya* is equivalent to reaching the state of samadhi, which in Yoga Nidra is reached through the back door.

The rest produced by Yoga Nidra is equivalent to hours of ordinary sleep, and when the technique is mastered it can replace it.

The practice we do in Yoga Nidra is equivalent to the practice of the witness we do in everyday life, keeping ourselves in consciousness without identifying ourselves with its contents. It is the paradigm of Kriya Yoga, Nityananda: the constant joy that arises from being in the witness, the Seer of Patanjali, the Self that we are.

So-Ham meditation

Every time we breath in, we repeat SO (He, the universal Self) and every time we breathe out, we repeat AHAM (I, the individual ego). Thus, we urge the individual ego to realize the Self supreme. The SO while inhaling and AHAM while exhaling form the sacred sentence SOHAM which means "I am He." "I am Bliss Eternal."

- The Voice of Babaji[1]

You can do japa with the breath. This will be ajapa-japa of SOHAM. Repeat mentally SO with inhalation and HAM with exhalation.

- The Voice of Babaji[2]

This meditation is very simple and powerful because it also integrates and relaxes the breath. You can record it, keeping a ten-minute pause between the first and second paragraph, and then listen to the recording when you start meditating:

"We sit in comfortable posture, with a straight back and eyes closed. We just watch our breath, how the air enters and how it comes out. **It is very important not to direct or control our breathing;** we only watch it happen by itself. As our body inhales we mentally repeat the sound **SO**, and as we exhale, we mentally repeat the sound **HAM**. We only do that. If any thoughts come, we let them pass by, as if they were birds that cross the sky, and we return to focus on our breathing. SO when the body inhales and HAM when the body exhales. We let about 10 minutes go by.

Now, while still doing the above, we also observe the brief natural pause that occurs after the end of exhalation and the beginning of the next inhalation. It is a natural moment of silence (in Yoga it is called "*kumbhaka*") in which there is no breathing. We also observe this natural moment without breathing and notice the peace and calm that emanate from it. We can notice that, as our mind and our breathing relax more and more, this moment becomes longer and longer - but we continue without forcing or directing the breath, we just observe it and follow it with the sound SO-HAM.

We may also notice that bliss is emanating from that moment of pause. Bliss is a joy that arises regardless of external circumstances. Focus more and more on this bliss. Notice it in your plexus, notice that it radiates and expands throughout your body.

That bliss you notice is your inner space of bliss. It is the unconditioned joy of your Self. It is always available to you through your practice. Allow yourself to enjoy it more and more, without reservation. Expand yourself in this endless bliss, let it fill you and heal you. Stay in this state as long as you want. When you finish the meditation, allow this bliss to remain with you wherever you go. When you finish the meditation, you will allow this joy to remain with you wherever you go".

You can prolong the meditation as long as you want.

When you finish the meditation, bring to your daily life the bliss obtained with the practice.

The mental repetition of a mantra or divine sound along with the breath is called "*ajapa japa*". Some yogis practice the *ajapa* of So-Ham throughout the day, with each breath, as a way of realizing the Self; this practice was followed and mastered by some Siddhas.

1- *The Voice of Babaji*, p. 165.
2- Id., p. 482.

The sadhana of the chakras in Kriya Yoga

In Babaji's Kriya Yoga we offer the prayer of dedication prior to the practices of the kriyas of the chakras. Each chakra is tuned with Babaji (not with deities, as in other tantric Yogas); when the sadhaka focus on the chakra he surrenders it to Him. In an advanced sadhana this tunes the chakras with the Satguru, and facilitates the surrender to and identification with our true Self. It reflects the admonition: *"Seek Babaji to become Babaji."*

The work of activation of the chakras is carried out progressively. It begins at the first initiation with the practice of the 18 asanas and *Kriya Kundalini Pranayama*. In the second initiation, the mantras of each of them are taught, and in the third initiation, advanced techniques are taught that include postures, mantras and meditations on the chakras.

Meditating on a chakra per day, for example, is fine - and tuning it with Babaji. Thus, we prepare the ground for the manifestation of a divine consciousness. This also purifies and dismantles the structure of the ego. By tuning the chakras with Babaji we gradually remove past conditioning, those tendencies and habits which manifest egoism and create suffering. The positive activation of the higher chakras in particular will put them in the driver's seat of our approach to life's challenges. It is a process that takes time and requires constant and patient practice from the sadhak.

About the kriyas of samadhi

The samadhi kriyas are learned in the third initiation of Babaji's Kriya Yoga. It is necessary to be well established in the practice of Kriya to develop their potential.

Our consciousness is our greatest treasure. The practice of the kriyas of samadhi can deepen it and expand it.

Those sadhaks who follow a more devotional approach on the path of union with the Divine can consider these kriyas as alternative ways to experience Babaji in a personal form: Babaji as silence, as light, as absolute unity, as divine sound.

In preparation for practice of the samadhi kriyas, numbered 139, 140, 141 and 144, it is advisable to to have some mastery or siddhi of the kriyas taught previously. While they can all be practiced together, just as with the practices of the 7 meditations of the first initiation, mastery of the first techniques ensures better progress in the following techniques.

It is always useful to meditate with the Satguru to receive guidance on those practices that are most appropriate for each student in each moment.

#139 Om Babaji Sarvikalpa Samadhi Kriya

In the second initiation the student learns to practice verbal silence, *mouna*. Now with this kriya we learn to enter mental silence with the help of breath. The Self is unconditional joy, bliss or Ananda. The delusionary power in the ordinary mind, by which the One appears to be many, and there appears to be limitations of time, knowledge, power, karma and passion is known as *maya*. The mind is like a broken mirror in which the Self multiplies itself. But the Self does not cease to be, even deformed by the perturbations of the mind. These perturbations are like dirt on the surface of a mirror, and prevent us from seeing the underlying reality of absolute being, consciousness and bliss in the world. Stillness of the mind suspends its perturbations, and at this moment the joyful rays of Self filter through the mind. By reaching the *siddhi* (mastery) of this technique, the state of absorption in pure consciousness is experienced at will, beyond the mind, which eventually gives way to Nirvikalpa samadhi, the union without any differentiation. In the path of the Siddhas this realization of samadhi must then be brought to the rest of our bodies or sheaths, including the physical.

Just as mastery of the Shuddi Dhyana Kriya technique creates the basis for the other meditations, the practice and mastery of kriya #139 creates the basis for the other kriyas of samadhi. This kriya creates a space of stillness so that a higher consciousness can descend. Focus on creating that base of peace. Do this kriya as long as it takes until you feel that consolidated base.

It is important to keep awareness present and awake when practicing it, avoiding sleep or evasion. If daydreaming or subliminal thoughts appear, detachment from them should be practiced. Little by little the sadhaka will enter into deeper and deeper states of stillness and peace without falling asleep or losing consciousness.

In the practice of this kriya the student sometimes soon enters a state of absorption. At other times his practice is prolonged until there comes a time when breathing is released and relaxed and the student enters a joyful state of peace. The latter can sometimes take an hour of practice to happen, but the joyful and peaceful state can be prolonged throughout the day.

If this practice is accompanied by the cleansing of the subconscious with Shuddi or detachment and the work on the chakras and the 9 openings, the evolution of the other techniques of samadhi (kriyas #140, #141, #144) will be natural, which can then manifest their full potential. Otherwise the mind can produce interruptions and even wide detours which may take you away from the sadhana.

So, work with this kriya again and again until the stillness of the breath and of the mind become your natural state, and the rays of peace and the intuition of the Self could manifest through this stillness. And then, at the end of the meditation, try to take this stillness into your daily life.

With the practice of this kriya, stillness and blissful peace without modifications (thoughts or feelings) must become the second nature of the student. Reaching this state is a great yogic realization; this space of stillness allows a higher consciousness to arise. And yet there are more realizations from this state, which are achieved with the other kriyas of samadhi.

#140 Soruba (Purna) Jyoti Samadhi Dhyana Kriya

To advance in this kriya it is necessary not to disperse sexual energies and to have transmuted much vital energy into spiritual, through bandhas and *Brahmacharya Ojas Maitreka Pranayama*. This energy transmuted into upper chakras allows the vision of internal light. The siddhi of this technique produces the opening of the *Ajna* chakra between the eyebrow and the experience of the divine light of Shiva or Self, widely mentioned in the Siddhas texts. This experience of the divine light has different levels - the Tirumandiram speaks of them - the highest culminates with the descent of the light of Grace into the cells of the body, culminating in what is referred to as *soruba samadhi*.

When doing this practice, meditate on the Divine as an omnipresent light and feel that all that exists is the manifestation of this light. Meditate on the light, on Chidambaram and on the lineage of the Siddhas (see chapter "The center of the eyebrows and the vision of the light").

#141 Nirvikalpa Samadhi Dhyana Kriya

- *The only sadhana to obtain Nirvikalpa Samadhi is Para*

Vairagya (supreme detachment).
- Here the yogi is completely disconnected from Prakriti (nature) and its effects.
- The mind, intellect and senses cease to function completely.
- There are no sounds or contacts or shapes here.

- Swami Sivananda[1]

Reaching the *siddhi* of this kriya means attaining the realization of Self, Satchidananda. This kriya requires the previous activation of all the chakras in order to be carried out in a sustainable way, a great cleaning of the subconscious (chitta) and a complete surrender to the Satguru. The *prana* will naturally concentrate on the crown chakra when all impediments to its ascent such as attachments and aversions, have been removed.

For the Siddhas, unlike Classical Yoga, nirvikalpa samadhi is not necessarily the exit door from of the manifested world; it can also be the door of descent of the Divine into all five bodies including the physical body in *soruba samadhi* or divinization of all lower bodies (see the chapter "The center of the crown and Ultimate Oneness").

#144 – Shayvie Omkara Nada Dhyana Kriya

The One decided to become many, in its freedom and joyful expression. In its love for the many, it gives each of us the freedom to experience separation, and if and when a soul seeks Oneness, it graciously and lovingly leads it home to its embrace in samadhi. Between the One and the many is the cosmic vibration of the Om, which generates all the multiplicity. The yogi tunes with Om's omnipresent vibration, listens to it and absorbs it, and then begins to feel and experience that unique Presence that is everywhere. The Om thus becomes the way back to the One.

In the beginning was the Word, and the Word was with God,

and the Word was God. He was in the beginning with God. All things were made through him, and without him was not anything made that was made.

- John 1.1-4

He danced as manifest sound, the dance of eternal sound.

- Tirumandiram 2751

Listening to the Om sound as a practice of meditation for the realization of Self is in different Yoga lineages.

The sounds are heard in the pure space
Take rest! Sleep within the sound
Gaining the sleep of pure consciousness.

- Siddha Konkanavar[2]

The sadhaka reaches the *siddhi* of this technique when he is able to hear *Nada*, the divine sound of Om, without closing the ears. Absorption in this divine sound produces different levels of absorption or samadhi, and it is a source of joy; another name of this technique is "*Nadanda Yoga*" - the blis of divine sound. The absorption in the Om sound also aims to bring us to its source, what the Siddhas call *Nadanta* (that which is beyond Nada or divine sound Om) - that is the state of *turiya*, the primordial consciousness that gives rise to the other states of consciousness.

The end of sound, the end of knowledge,
The end of the Vedas, the true bliss of Siva,
The blemishless, virtuous Sadasiva-ananda
Is the dance of the nada-brahman of siva.

- Tirumandiram 2792

In Babaji's Kriya Yoga we practice listening to Om in Ida, Pingala and Sushumna, and finally in the center of the heart.

1- Sivananda, Swami. (2007). *Fourteen Lessons on Raja Yoga. Divine Life Society.*
2- *The Yoga of the 18 Siddhas*, p. 151.

Steps in advancing in Babaji's Kriya Yoga

One cannot evaluate one's own spiritual advancement, but the sadhaka can consider to what extent he advances in these different progressive steps of sadhana. In Babaji's Kriya Yoga, the effective practice of many techniques requires the some mastery of previous techniques. Sometimes we do not advance in certain parts of the practice because we have not advanced in the previous practices.

The student can consider his progress in the following steps of the path of Kriya Yoga and discover in which one of the steps he or she requires more practice to keep on advancing in the path:

- An established practice of asanas (and bandhas) as a basis of stability and physical, emotional and mental well-being.

- Mastery of *Shuddi Dhyana Kriya*. This is undoubtedly the cornerstone on which the entire building of the practice of Kriya Yoga is built. The mastery of detachment, correctly carried out, especially on conflicting emotions, is a great yogic *siddhi*, necessary for the realization of Self:

The first and the most essential preparation for a real aspirant seeking the spiritual goal is vairagya *(detachment). (...)* Vairagya *is not an escape from the objects, but a conquest of the objects. It is born of strength of mind and not weakness of the will.*

- The voice of Babaji[1]

Mastery of detachment over conflicting emotions means advancing beyond the disturbances of the lower chakras.

- Creating a guide and inspiration channel with the Satguru through the seventh meditation of the First Initiation.

- Mastery of Nityananda Kriya, the blissful witness; the practice of Presence and Love daily life.

- Devotional practices of Kriya Bhakti Yoga as a means of cultivating aspiration for the True, the Good, the beautiful, unconditional love, surrender, and the transmutation of difficult emotions.

- Surrender of all actions to the Satguru. Consecration of all actions to the internal guide. Seeing everything that happens as the play of the Divine creation for the edification and evolution of our soul in wisdom and realization.

- Receiving guidance and inspiration from the 18 Siddhas.

- Unconditional service to others, Karma Yoga, as a way to open the heart and to release the energy and inspiration created through the yogic practice.

- Preservation and transmutation of sexual energy, avoiding loss of seminal fluids.

- Mastery of the concentration in a single point (second and fifth meditations of the first initiation).

- Activation and purification of the chakras; mental and emotional cleansing of their samskaras through of the practice of detachment (kriyas 102 to 122, plus kriya # 82, *Mandira Matreika Pranayama*).

- Purification of nine openings; mental and emotional cleansing of their samskaras through the practice of detachment (kriyas 123 to 131).

- Mastery of kriya #139, *Om Babaji Sarvikalpa Samadhi Kriya*.

- Practice and mastery of the rest of the kriyas of samadhi.

3- *The Voice of Babaji*, p. 202-203.

Glossary of terms

Agni: the internal fire, the energy generated in the third chakra, Manipura, related to the fire element.

Ajapa: the mental repetition of a mantra or divine name in sync with the natural inhalation and exhalation of the body.

Ananda: bliss; joy; a quality of the Self, which is unconditional.

Ashram: the residence of a yogi.

Bandhas: muscular locks practiced in Hatha Yoga that redirect energy and facilitate the activation of chakras and kundalini energy.

Bhakti Yoga: the Yoga of union with the Self through love and devotion.

Bindu: semen, vital essence; seed; starting point.

Brahman: the impersonal divine principle which is the origin of everything; absolute being, consciousness and bliss.

Chakras: literally, "wheels;" subtle psycho-energy centers that are distributed in the human body.

Chitta: mental substance, including the deep subconscious.

Dharma: the principle of righteousness, of what is right and appropriate by nature, not as an imposed norm; our proper task or mission in life.

Granthi: energy knot that must be removed to achieve full spiritual development.

Guru: literally, "he who dispels the darkness;" teacher and spiritual guide; he who teaches how to transcend the influence of the gunas or modes of nature.

Japa: mental repetition of the name of God.

Karma: the consequences of action, words and thoughts, which can be negative or positive, causing suffering or unhappiness to oneself or others.

Karma Yoga: the Yoga of union with the Self through the selfless action offered to the Divine.

Koshas: the five sheaths or envelopes that conceal the Self: physical, emotional or vital, mental, intellectual and spiritual.

Kriya: literally "action with consciousness;" yogic technique.

Kumbhaka: the moment of pause that occurs in breathing, without inhalation or exhalation of air.

Kundalini: divine force; our potential psycho-spiritual energy, symbolized as a coiled snake sitting at the base of the column that once awakened, rises through various subtle centers (chakras) located in the column, to reach the crown of the head, producing union with the Self; our potential of consciousness and energy that can be awakened through the Yoga practices.

Mantras: sacred syllables or divine sounds, transmitted by realized masters, which generate a higher energy and consciousness in those who repeat them.

Maya: the cosmic deception that divides the Self, the One, into an infinite multiplicity.

Mouna: the yogic practice of keeping silence.

Nada: the divine sound Om.

Nadanta: that which is beyond *nada*, the divine sound; its source.

Nadis: subtle channels of energy or prana.

Ojas: spiritual energy.

Om: the vibration or divine sound that gives for to all creation.

Prana: vital energy.

Pranayama: Yoga techniques that use breathing to achieve

various physical, emotional and mental effects.

Prarabdha karma: the unavoidable karma of one's life; one's destiny

Sadhak: the one who practices sadhana.

Sadhana: practice or spiritual discipline.

Samadhi: cognitive absorption, mental silence, breathless state of union with the Absolute.

Samsara: the endless wheel of rebirths.

Samskaras: trends and habits stored in the subconscious mind.

Satguru: supreme guru.

Shakti: energy; divine energy.

Shiva: the Lord, the Absolute; the supreme consciousness.

Siddha: perfected beings; the realized masters who developed the scientific art of Yoga.

Siddhi: perfection, dominion; yogic power.

Soruba samadhi: the final realization of the Siddhas, in which the physical body gets divinized.

Tapas: very intense yogic practice.

Tattvas: the different principles of nature.

Turiya: the primordial state of consciousness, the foundation of the other states: wakefulness, dreaming and dreamless sleep.

Vasanas: tendencies to dwell on particular pleasant or unpleasant memories.

Vettaveli: in Tamil, inner vast luminous space of consciousness; the Siddha's favorite description of the Supreme Being.

Yantras: symbolic drawings that are used to meditate and invoke divine aspects or Siddhas.

Yoga: Ancient philosophy, psychology and practice of India,

conducive to a healthy and harmonious living and the realization of Self.

Bibliography

- Aurobindo, Sri. (2005). *Letters on Yoga*. Pondicherry: Sri Aurobindo Ashram Publications Department.

- Aurobindo, Sri. (2014). *Letters on Yoga III*. Pondicherry: Sri Aurobindo Ashram Publications Department

- Aurobindo, Sri. (2015). *Letters on Yoga IV*. Pondicherry: Sri Aurobindo Ashram Publications Department.

- Aurobindo, Sri. (1997). *Savitri: A legend and a symbol*. Pondicherry: Sri Aurobindo Ashram Publication Department.

- Aurobindo, Sri. (2003). *The integral Yoga*. Twin Lakes, USA: Lotus Press.

- Aurobindo, Sri. (2012). *The Mother with Letters on the Mother*. Pondicherry: Sri Aurobindo Ashram Publications Department.

- Ayyapa Giri, S. (2014). *Samadhi Secrets of the Himalayan Mahavatar Babaji*. http://kalipath.com/?p=10.

- Chandra Vasu, S. (translator). (1914). *Siva Samhita*. Allahabad: The Panini Office, Bhuvanesware Asrama, Bahadurganj.

- Doshi, N. (1974). *Guidance from Sri Aurobindo, Letters to a Young Disciple. Volume 1*. Auroville: Sri Aurobindo Ashram Trust.

- Ganapathy, T.N. (1993). *The philosophy of the Tamil Siddhas*. New Delhi: Indian Council of Philosophical Research

- Ganapathy, T. N. (2003). *The Yoga of Siddha Boganathar Vol. 1*. St. Etienne de Bolton, Québec: Babaji's Kriya Yoga and Publications.

- Ganapathy, T. N. (Ed.). (2004). *The Yoga of the 18 Siddhas: An anthology*. St. Etienne de Bolton, Quebec: Babaji's

Kriya Yoga and Publications.

- Govindan, M. (1993). *Babaji and the 18 Siddha Kriya Yoga tradition.* St. Etienne de Bolton, Quebec: Babaji's Kriya Yoga and Publications.

- Govindan, M. (2010). *Kriya Yoga Sutras of Patanjali and the Siddhas: Translation, Commentary and Practice.* St. Etienne de Bolton, Quebec: Babaji's Kriya Yoga and Publications.

- Little, L. Shaking the Tree: *Kundalini Yoga, Spiritual Alchemy, & the Mysteries of the Breath in Bhogar's 7000.* Disponible en https://www.alchemywebsite.com/bhogar.html

- Mahendra Baba, Mahendra, Shastriji, Babaji. *Sri Sadashiv Charitamrit.* (Traducción provisional).

- Mother, the. (2003). *Questions and Answers 1929-1931.* Pondicherry: Sri Aurobindo Ashram Publications Department.

- Mother, the. (2004). *Words of the Mother III.* Pondicherry: Sri Aurobindo Ashram Publications Department.

- Neelakantan, V.T.N., Ramaiah, S.A.A., y Nagaraj, Babaji. (2003). *The Voice of Babaji; a trilogy of Kriya Yoga.* St. Etienne de Bolton, Quebec: Babaji's Kriya Yoga and Publications.

- Ramaiah, S.A.A. (2019). *Tamil Kriya Yoga Siddhantham – Homes.* Available in:

https://babajiskriyayogalecturesofyogisaaramaiah.simplecast.fm/13c0f6f1

- Shri Haidakhan Babaji's Online Ashram. *The Teachings of Babaji 1979-1984.* Disponible en:

https://www.truthsimplicitylove.com/

- Tirumular Siddhar. (2010). *The Tirumandiram.* St. Etienne de Bolton, Québec: Babaji´s Kriya Yoga and Publications.

- Vanmikanathan, G. (1976). *Pathway to God Trod by Saint Ramalingar.* Bombay: Bharatiya Vidya Bhavan. Disponible en:

http://www.vallalar.org/English/V000009431B.

Made in the USA
Las Vegas, NV
18 April 2024

88809321R00079